C000194537

CHANGE ME!

Samuel C Cowgill

Published by Litnum Publications
22 Hillcrest Avenue, Scarborough
North Yorkshire YO12 6RQ
www.litnumpublications.co.uk

All rights reserved. No part of this publication may be reproduced or stored in a retrieval system, or transmitted, in any form or by any means, electronic, mechanical, photocopying, recording or otherwise without the prior written permission of the author, nor be otherwise circulated in any form of binding or cover other than in which it is published. The right of Samuel Conroy Cowgill to be identified as the author of this work has been asserted by him in accordance with the Copyright Design and Patents Act 1988.

© Copyright 2014 Samuel Conroy Cowgill

British Library Cataloguing in Publication Data
A catalogue record for this book is available from the British Library.

ISBN 978-0955-7664-6-6

Unless otherwise stated all Scripture quotations are taken from the Holy Bible, New International Version Anglicised Copyright © 1979, 1984, 2011 Biblica, formerly International Bible Society

Used by permission of Hodder & Stoughton Publishers, an Hachette UK company
All rights reserved
'NIV' is a registered trademark of Biblica
UK trademark number 1448790.

Cover design and type set by S C Cowgill

Printed and bound by
CPI Group (UK) Ltd, Croydon, CR0 4YY

Acknowledgements

I truly thank my Creator God for His grace offered to me through Jesus and for the gift of His Holy Spirit. I give my Heavenly Father glory for equipping, directing and being with me throughout the good and tough times I faced when writing this book. Without His love, patience, and continuing presence, I could not have completed the work.

I extend my gratitude to Angelo for letting me share his journey and more so, for helping me draw closer to Jesus. My heartfelt thanks go to John and Gill Payne, Ivan Squillino and Rob for their encouragement.

I must thank Marina, Ali, Imran and Luciana (pseudonyms) for their unfailing love, support, and willingness to speak of their relationship with Jesus.

Thanks go to Sheena Beadle, Doreen Brown, Gwyneth Riley, Heather Rowe, Neville Smith and Ruth Taylor for reading and commenting on the interim draft.

I thank Margaret Harris for giving freely of her time to proof read the various drafts.

Special thanks go to my wife, Veronica for her patience in spending many lonely hours while I was writing.

Contents

Acknowledgements..3

Impressionable and Gullible...5

Loneliness and Temptation 15

An Unnerving Event 27

Joy and Heartache..35

A Break in the Darkness 41

Two Friends..52

The Past: Forgiven and Forgotten.....................................65

Real or Just a Fad...77

Renegade 94

The Promise.. 105

The Other Woman 112

Blessings and Conflicts... 119

Doing His Will.. 131

Not Alone 140

Telling Others... 150

In His Care.. 158

God's Timing... 169

Living the Word 180

Keen to Serve 190

Disturbing News 197

Love and Pride 204

Under Attack 217

Angelo's thoughts about asking Jesus into your life 232

Author's Notes 235

1

Impressionable and Gullible

A dark haired and brown eyed bearded Italian paced his bedroom; cursing the English weather. 'Ten minutes, that's all I've got,' he snapped, checking his wristwatch. His desperation heightened when the rain thrashed the windows. Downing the remains of a can of beer, he grabbed his jacket and peaked hat to brave the storm.

'Hi Angelo,' called out a friend passing by.

Too intense to reply or notice the sun breaking through the clouds as the rain turned to a light drizzle, his thoughts were distant. 'I'll win this time. I'm sure of it,' he mumbled.

Angelo was no stranger to the gamblers' dining table. Enticed by the excitement of winning and forgetful of the sadness of losing, he'd been a regular at the betting shop. Often he'd risked his entire earnings on a horse and then frittered away his winnings on bad bets before scurrying home; deflated at the loss of his hard-earned money. As always, the bitterness of losing quickly faded as visions of beating the bookie's odds stirred his imagination. Keen to place his bet, he rushed on; convinced his next wager would roll in the cash.

This time would be different. He could feel it in his bones and bubbling in his veins. 'Just one more bet will set me right,' he muttered; unaware of others passing by and that the rain had stopped.

The betting shop was his sanctuary, a place to hide and escape from a broken marriage and the heavy workload of his restaurant. These were just excuses.

He'd been divorced for years and his restaurant was doing well.

Day after day, he'd played the machines, put a few pounds on the horses and challenged the bookie's odds on favourites by placing his bets on outsiders. He enjoyed the thrill of an adrenaline rush, a pounding heart and the warm glow of feeling high. *Win the bet* became his battle cry. An innocent looking pastime had become a compulsive fix; a craving he denied when challenged.

He loved the times when he won. 'Yes!' he would shout; abandoning his inhibitions as others nearby shared his euphoria. He hated losing. There was no elation, especially when dropping his spent betting slips into the bin, hoping no one had noticed.

Rushing along the street, failed bets were far from Angelo's thoughts. Anxiously fingering his pockets, he stopped in his tracks. 'I've lost it.' His heart pounding, he tried desperately to recall where he'd stuffed his wallet packed with twenties, tens and fives. 'Found it,' he sighed, touching the leather pouch. His anxiety gone, excitement likened to huge waves crashed over him at the thought of winning. Beaming with enthusiasm, he reached the betting shop door but no further. It was as though a steel shutter, impenetrable yet transparent, had dropped between him and the entrance. He tried to step forward, but could not move. Fearful as to what was happening to him, he reeled in anger.

Almost twenty-seven years earlier, Angelo had arrived in England as a mere twenty year old. One of three sons, born in a north-westerly Italian coastal town, he'd spent his formative years playing around or running errands for his mum and dad. Like most Italians educated in Italy, he'd attended the local church school. As he grew older, he shied away from anything with religious overtones; confining church attendance to births, marriage and deaths.

At an impressionable age, he wondered what he would do for a living and more so what he would be. He dreamt of becoming a footballer but soon dropped the idea when picturing himself kicking his way past much taller fellows to score a goal. He fancied himself as an actor, and persuaded his mum to take him to an audition in Rome. His acting ambitions ended abruptly when, following the audition, the promoter demanded a backhander to help advance his career. Angelo's mum refused to part with a single lira. Other desires took his fancy. Like football and acting, his dreams came to nothing. One day he read a brochure about London and pictured himself riding around the capital on a red bus. From then on, he developed a yearning to learn the English language and to experience living in Britain.

He left school at fifteen without a single qualification. He had no idea what work he would do and neither did he care. A rebel, he drifted into catering by working in his mum and dad's restaurant, baking, cooking and serving at tables. By the time military service raised its head, he confessed he'd never read the Bible and held no faith. To him religion was a waste of time; corrupt and not worthy of consideration.

His dad was no saint. He shared his son's view as far as religion was concerned. Like Angelo, he too had no time for such nonsense; as he understood it to be. Of average build, hair almost black and clean-shaven,

Angelo's dad was a man of few words. His piercing eyes were enough to say all he needed to convey, especially when directing his penetrating glare towards his children. Of Sicilian descent, when younger he'd been involved in dubious activities, living amidst a gangland culture. Forsaking former things, laying aside his knife and gun, he fixed his thoughts on providing for his family and moved to mainland Italy. An extremely hard worker, he drank heavily, swore a lot and occasionally exhibited his temper. Like many fathers who struggled hard in the post war era to adjust to civilian life, he remained somewhat remote from his sons; but in his way, he loved them deeply. Up by four a.m. to clean the restaurant, replenish stocks and prepare food, he would work until one a.m. which meant he spent little time with his children.

Angelo's sweetheart was his mum, whom he loved deeply. She was as much a hard worker as his dad, and perhaps more so by holding the family together in turbulent times; especially when her spouse's social drinking became obsessive. His mum was the eldest of six daughters and the mainstay of the family; caring for her sisters in difficult circumstances. Angelo's Sicilian grandparents were market traders selling fresh fruit.

At the age of twenty, Angelo's dream of visiting Britain became a reality. He jumped at the chance when a family friend invited him to work for six months in his Italian restaurant in England; mainly over the winter period. Since undertaking National Service, Angelo's life had been one huge downward spiral. Living with his parents was not the cause of his waywardness. He loved his family. Aware that others were grooming him for illegal activities, it was highly likely he'd have slipped into a life of crime; had he not left Italy at that time.

The restaurant in Britain could have been on the moon for all Angelo cared. Out came his maps. There it was; a northern town on the east coast of England. The opportunity for him to see Britain and speak the language had arrived. Not that he could say a word of English! Such words as 'okay' and 'hi' were all he knew, and they were not of British origin. Despite his minor language barrier and a fear of flying - for he'd never been in an aircraft - he was excited at the prospects of a new beginning and looked forward to the adventure. With great excitement, one fine October day, he packed a small case, tucked his passport and work permit into his pocket, kissed his mum a fond farewell and headed to the airport with a friend.

Angelo didn't like the idea of being thousands of feet in the air. He closed his eyes on take-off, bravely opening them when airborne. It took him a while to relax. There were many scary moments as the plane frequently hit air pockets. When not terrified by turbulence, he gazed from the window across a sea of clouds. The constant droning of the engines slowly lulled him into a dreamy state. He sank back in his seat, closed his eyes and thought of home. In a semi-dazed state, he recalled the time when, as a sprightly seven year old he was kicking a can across the cobbled street near his dad's restaurant. Next door stood a delicatessen shop packed with sweets and chocolates.

'Hey, Angelo!' beckoned his dad appearing at the restaurant door waving a small paper bag.

Thankful for something to do, and more so for somewhere to go, he kicked the can into the gutter and ran across the cobbles.

'Take these sandwiches to Mrs Giuseppe.'

'I will, Papa.' Off he ran down the street towards the cinema. On reaching the church, he spied an unkempt drunken man struggling up the steps.

'Get away! Get away!' bellowed a short stocky priest appearing at the church doorway shooing the bedraggled fellow off the premises.

The man continued to stagger up the steps. Stumbling to his knees, he lifted pleading hands towards the priest.

'Off! Go on! Get away from this place!' demanded the priest dashing from the church.

Angelo, a perceptive and sensitive boy, watched as the cleric dragged the man by his collar down the steps, throwing him into the gutter. Brushing his hands in great satisfaction, the pious fellow dashed into the church slamming the door. The outcast, too drunk to stand, struggled to rise. Unable to do so, he sobbed bitterly.

Angelo's compassion for the stranger overwhelmed him. *That's not right. If that's how the church treats people, I'll not go there. Not likely.* He wanted to give him the sandwiches his dad had made, but thought better of it when picturing what might happen to him on returning home. He stood for a while eyeing the sobbing man and then with a twinge of guilt at deserting him, ran to the cinema. He remained upset when handing the sandwiches to the proprietor. 'My dad sent you these.'

'Thank you, Angelo,' she smiled. 'You can watch the film if you want. It's just about to start.'

Needing no encouragement, he slipped into the stalls just in time to see the title flash across the screen.

Suddenly the heavy turbulence wrenched him from his dreaming. A few stressful hours passed before Angelo landed on British soil. After collecting his luggage and passing through passport control and customs, the coldness of a grey autumn day hit him hard. Gone was the temperate climate he loved. He stood on unfamiliar ground. The flight and the hassle of crossing London along with the rail journey up the east coast took its toll. Fatigued, and only one hour away from his final destination, fog shrouded the land. He was not happy when greeted by his employer. 'It's so cold. I'm shivering.'

Speaking in Italian when walking Angelo and his friend to the car, 'You'll soon get used to it,' laughed his boss. 'Did you have a good journey?'

'The flight was not good,' he replied. 'There was a lot of turbulence. I slept most of the way.'

The luggage safely stowed, he peered from the car window wondering if he'd made a mistake by visiting England. Cold, damp and grey, fog was not what he'd seen back home when scanning the brochures. The hour's journey stretched endlessly into four as the fog thickened. Reaching the restaurant, his boss led him up numerous flights of stairs to the top flat.

'You'll be fine here. Rest for a while and then join me for a meal. I'll show you around the place later. The restaurant opens from ten until one o'clock and again at five until eleven thirty; seven days a week. You'll work for six.'

Angelo was too tired to care. Work did not bother him. He'd worked far longer hours in Italy. The room looked welcoming but it wasn't home. Things were different. The doors opened in the opposite direction to those in Italy and there were two basin taps on one sink and two on the bath. He was used to one mixer tap. All he wanted to do was wash and then sleep. Turning two taps to acquire the correct water temperature proved difficult. Abandoning his wash, he flung himself onto his bed; still wondering if England was a good choice. Gazing up at the skylight, he assured himself six months would soon pass.

He settled well into restaurant life. It was much like home except for the difference in speech. Learning a new language is difficult at the best of times. Trying to grasp the peculiarities of the local vernacular was hard enough for Angelo. Hearing the variant ways of pronouncing the same word when spoken by folks visiting from the industrial cities west of the county proved to be challenging. Then there were the regional Scottish accents and differing accentuated tones of the coastal regions to the north. *I'll never learn this language. It's crazy; too many words meaning the same thing.*

He conceded that learning a new language, seeing new things and observing cultural differences was part of the game. What he loathed most, especially when trying to sleep, was the constant squawking of seagulls walking across the skylight.

The work was hard, but enjoyable. He soon got used to serving roughly four hundred people each night. To

Angelo, the town was like stepping back in time with its castle ruins set back on a high peninsula. The small terraced houses, fashionable sixteenth century mini mansions, and narrow cobbled streets tucked into the cleft of the hill overlooking the harbour fascinated him; a far contrast to his birthplace of modern developments. As the weeks slipped by; his fondness for the place grew. He loved watching the ebb and flow of the sea, washing over the sand almost reaching the promenade and the contrasting turbulent waves crashing against the sea wall beyond the old toll road. The thing he missed most was his mum's cooking.

Like many other workers who grab a little respite between shifts, Angelo was no exception. Working three hours and then a four-hour break before working a further five hours proved irksome. Everything was fine until one fateful invitation. Between serving at table and entering the kitchen to pick up the food, there was time for a spot of Italian conversation.

'Fancy going to the betting shop?' asked his friend.

'What's that?'

'It's a place where we gamble. Horses, dogs, and the like.'

'Yeah, why not?'

After the morning shift, Angelo stuffed a few coins into his pocket and off he went to try his hand at winning a fortune. The simple invitation to pass a few hours on a seemingly innocent game posed no threat to him when entering the betting shop. His gambling started like most innocent activities. A few pence bet soon became two, three and hundreds and thousands of flawed expectations. The thrill of the challenge to prove himself rang sweet in his ears when collecting his winnings. The sheer annoyance and depressive effects of losing were hard to swallow. The urge to place one more bet and the need to feel the excitement of winning quickly took hold as the familiar phrase *'It's just a bit of fun. It's harmless'* began to blot out the true cost of his gaming.

2
Loneliness and Temptation

Angelo had been in England for almost a month when late autumn ushered in a cold spell prior to winter snow and ice. The trees shed their yellow and bronze leaves as the wind whisked them across the pavements into any nook and cranny. Dark nights lengthened, bringing a heightened awareness of how draughty the flat had suddenly become. Angelo was grateful for the small electric fire that belted out its heat as he tried to keep warm. The camaraderie with his work colleagues brought little comfort. The early hours were the worst. Lying in his bed far from home, cold, lonely, and not yet able to converse adequately in the indigenous language, he let self-pity fill his mind. Desperate to keep warm, he tucked the bedclothes beneath his chin, closed his eyes and thought of home. Taking refuge in the imaginary warm Mediterranean breeze kissing his cheeks, he indulged in his fantasy; unaware that a sudden awakening of a dormant memory can herald distortions rather than faithful facts. Sinking his head into his pillow, childhood memories of home and the friendly act of a neighbour awakened his imagination.

'I've brought something nice for you to take to Summer School,' smiled the genteel woman from the delicatessen shop next-door.

As a mere seven year old, Angelo's eyes widened and his mouth watered at the sight of so many packets of sweets and chewing gum. 'Fantastic! I'll pack them in my suitcase,' he said, grateful for the gifts.

'Don't eat them all at once,' warned his mum. 'I don't want you to be ill while you're away.'

'I'll eat a few each day,' he smiled. 'There might not be any there.'

'Of course there will,' assured his mum. 'From what the priest tells me, you'll be well looked after. There'll be lots of food, ice cream and fruit juice for you to enjoy. You'll have a lovely time in Valle d' Aosta. It won't be all lessons. I'm told you'll have lots of trips out and exciting things to learn and see. You'll enjoy it so much you'll not want to come home.'

Spending time in the picturesque Italian Alps caught his imagination. He'd learned at school that Valle d' Aosta, the smallest of the Italian regions, was the least populous and had cold winters and cool summers. He looked forward to seeing Mont Blanc [Monte Bianco] and the Matterhorn [Monte Cervino] and perhaps visit Mont Blanc tunnel. He'd no heart for study when on holiday. Studying arithmetic, Italian grammar, geography and performing religious observances were not his idea of having a good time.

'I'll help with your things,' smiled the friendly neighbour carrying Angelo's suitcase to the transit van. A fond wave to his mum, he was away with friends. He had not quite grasped how long he'd be away from home. The 296 kilometres drive to the Aosta Province bordering Switzerland and France took hours. Tired from the long journey through mountain passes of scenic beauty and green valleys, the young travellers wondered if they'd ever reach their destination. Eventually the van weaved its way through the town of Aosta.

'We're here,' announced the driver; passing through the school iron gates and pulling up alongside numerous cars and coaches filled with equally boisterous boys and girls of Angelo's age.

With expectant eyes, the jabbering pupils pushed their way towards the door to collect their cases and explore the place. Angelo was the last to pick up his belongings.

A formidable tiled roofed two-storey brick building fronted by a large tarmac play area and encircled by a high wire perimeter fence was to be his home for a number of weeks. The only greenery Angelo could see was across the road skirting a river.

A few girls caught his eye, but they were quickly ushered away by waiting nuns. His excitement on approaching the school evaporated when a rounded middle aged plainly dressed woman with glaring eyes and carrying a clipboard appeared at the school doorway. Standing like a tough sergeant major preparing to drill unsuspecting recruits, she blurted out a list of names amongst which was Angelo's. Struggling with his suitcase, he joined the boys gathered around her.

'Grab your possessions and follow me!' she bellowed loud enough to frighten the most robust child. The woman guided her flock into the school and along a corridor, passing the toilets, to a large military-style dormitory of twenty beds and fixed lockers. 'Choose a bed and stand by it!' she screeched. A couple of younger lads started crying. 'Stop your snivelling and do as I say!' Angelo dumped his suitcase beside a bed as the woman marched up and down yelling, 'Lift your cases onto your bed and open them! Quickly now! Quickly!'

Everyone except Angelo rushed to obey the woman. He wanted to run far away as he watched her ferret through each child's belongings, confiscating things not permissible. Amidst a surge of chatter, she eventually arrived at his bedside. Seeing his case on the floor, she towered menacingly over him. He glared back with equal ferocity. The room fell silent. Everyone looked his way.

'Don't tangle with me, boy,' she growled. 'Do as I say! Get that case onto your bed.' Angelo ignored her. Determined to exert her authority, inhaling slowly with shoulders raised, she scowled at him. Pointing to the case, she gave a mid-air jab and then glided her finger to the bed; repeating her action.

He got the message and capitulated when seeing one eye widen as the other closed. Furious at her smug dominant sigh, he struggled to lift his case onto the bed.

'Open it! I haven't got all day!' He flicked the catches and lifted the lid. Her eyes lit up. 'What have we here?' she asked waving the sweets and chewing gum at Angelo.

'They're mine. A neighbour gave them to me.'

'Not anymore,' she said, dropping them into an extra-large pocket of her garment.

With no money, and knowing his mum would not visit, he could not replace anything the woman stole.

Turning, she addressed her charges. 'Your meal is in five minutes. Unpack your things, wash your hands and don't be late. The dining hall is to the left down the corridor. The washroom is just beyond the door.'

The minute she'd gone, the boys scurried to store their belongings, visit the washroom and then head for the dining hall. Soon, the boys were with the girls tucking into a light meal of pasta followed by seasonal fruit. After the meal, enforced segregation was the rule. A trip to the toilet, a quick wash and then bed became the norm. Many daylight hours passed before darkness descended.

Peering over his blanket, Angelo was surprised to see the woman enter the dormitory. Wearing a heavily draped nightgown, nightcap and thick socks, she yelled, 'We'll have silence!' and then climbed into a bed near the door.

The first night passed without incident; apart from when the woman woke everyone up by shouting, 'Get back to bed, boy!' whenever anyone attempted to visit the toilet.

Following breakfast of fruit and one drink, amidst boisterous shouting, pushing and shoving, the boys clambered into the classroom to start formal lessons.

Angelo had hardly sat at a desk when the woman standing at the front of the classroom bellowed almost loud enough to shatter the windows, 'Silence, you lot! I demand silence! Do you hear?' There was a hushed response as the woman eyed her pupils. 'Tomorrow when you enter my classroom there'll be silence. Do you understand?' There were lots of nodding heads. 'Good! In your desk, there are a number of books. Choose one and read it to yourself.' Up went the desk lids amid a deluge of moans and groans. 'Silence!' she insisted, perching on a high stool behind a tall wooden desk, eyeing her charges. Order restored, she pulled from her pocket a packet of Angelo's chewing gum.

He was furious; and more so when she ripped off the outer packaging and slipped a piece into her mouth. 'This is war,' he mumbled believing he'd come to the wrong school. The theft of his belongings by someone in authority was not what he had expected. He'd a mind to tell the priest of her stealing but decided to keep his mouth shut when considering the consequences.

Angelo likened summer school to a prison without bars. Crushed were his prospects of enjoying a wonderful time. His mum had signed the papers. Three months was the contract. Three long months it would be.

Things got much worse when he discovered to his horror that his fluid allowance was two drinks per day - breakfast and teatime. At the height of summer the heat was bearable, but still there were many thirsty souls.

Despite dry lips and parched tongues, Summer School was not all bad. Angelo loved the trips out. He viewed them as a great escape. Seeing Mont Blanc and the Matterhorn would remain images in his mind's eye wherever he walked. Whenever possible, he was down by the river with others quenching his thirst. The surrounding area was pleasing to the eye; yet loneliness plagued him.

Weeks slipped by and then the inevitable happened. One particular night, he was desperate to relieve himself. He'd lain in bed for hours drawing up his knees and nipping his legs together trying hard not to wet the bed. Enough was enough. Barefoot he slipped silently from his bed and tiptoed towards the door. Suddenly the woman let out a huge snore. *Good, she's asleep.* Gently turning the door handle, he was set to reach the washroom.

'Where do you think you're going, boy? Back to bed!'

No escape or relief, he scurried back to bed nursing a heavy bladder. The hours to daybreak were long and agonising as the minutes to wash time ticked by far more slowly than they'd ever done before. On rising, he was the first to reach the privy.

The summer school held rigidly to a strict water ration. However, a pupil could earn favours or be penalised for wrongdoing. When a child was good they could, that evening, drink fruit juice and watch television with the girls. Angelo was never quite good enough to have that pleasure. Trouble even found him when out walking beyond the perimeter fence. He and his classmates were desperate for a drink. Seeing a cow trough fed by spring water, he jumped over the wall.

'Get your head out of there!' bellowed the custodian.

Enduring twelve gruelling weeks of lessons, walks, dehydration, enforced church attendance, sleepless nights and no television, Angelo finally returned home; glad to be away from that place.

'Do you want to go next year?' asked his mum.

'No thanks,' was his reply.

Deep in a deep in a dreamlike state, the heavy British rain pounding the skylight brought him back to reality with vengeance. The coldness of his sockless foot protruding from his blankets confirmed home was many miles away. Abandoning his recollections, Summer School would remain a vivid memory anchored deep in his mind. His sense of loneliness remained when staggering out of bed to wash, shave and prepare breakfast. In his need to seek comfort and feel loved, he'd done what so many do when separated from family and friends. He'd rekindled memories that served only to feed the isolation. Had he known Jesus, he would not have been alone; for Jesus said, *'And surely, I am with you always, to the very end of the age'* (Matthew 28:20). Angelo did not know Jesus, and had no desire to know Him or think about Him.

His first month in England passed quickly. Sadly, the lure of gambling had tightened its grip. No longer was it just a trip to the betting shop but also a regular visit to the casino. On his days off, he slept most of the time. Late night and early morning gambling became his lifestyle along with visits to the disco, sipping champagne and knocking back the beer. He often felt light-headed as the alcohol and smoky atmosphere dampened his reasoning and blurred his vision. The casino and disco were where he relaxed; safe amongst friends speaking his native tongue. One night, while drinking and making conversation above the music, out came his cigarettes.

'Here, have one of mine,' urged a friend. He hesitated on seeing the roughly rolled weed. His friend noted his questioning expression. 'They're just cigs.'

Angelo was no stranger to tobacco. He'd taken his first drag in Italy aged thirteen. It's a familiar story heard so many times as told by the regretful. At school, he and a couple of friends had drummed up a few liras to buy cigarettes. At that time, a particular brand could be bought in ones and twos; just enough for beginners to sample the weed. Well away from prying eyes, he lit his first cig. A quick drag, a few coughs and a touch of light-headedness accompanied by dryness of the throat followed. He was not impressed but persevered. His school-day prank soon became addictive as nicotine flooded his bloodstream.

The heavy beat of disco music, the searching multi-coloured lights flashing across the heads of those on the dance floor along with the free-flowing intoxicants and cordial company lured Angelo into a false sense of security.

'Go on. Try one,' urged others of his company.

'No thanks. I prefer my own.'

Pushing the cigarette at him and swaying to the beat of the music, his friend insisted. 'Don't be such a wimp. Try one.' Swearwords accompanied by frustrated anger followed.

The persistent badgering raised memories of earlier days when cannabis had tipped its hat to him. Undertaking his National Service in the Italian Army Catering Corps, his daily pay was the equivalent of twenty pennies. He had little cash to feed his daily habit of twenty smokes. Having spent time in the south of Italy learning how to cook, the army moved him north to cater for a small elite group of generals.

His fellow chefs were friendly; with the exception of a tall, broad-shouldered bully who delighted in belittling him in front of others. He preferred to keep his distance; despite sharing the same barrack room. After cooking, serving meals and cleaning the kitchen, there was little for the men to do. Mostly they sat around playing cards, talking, drinking and smoking. Angelo had no idea that boredom, like laziness, is a deadener of the mind. Neither did he know that when both are present they have a way of weakening resistance; making it harder to refuse things not usually acceptable when busy.

Following a hectic cooking session, the men returned to their quarters to relax. Angelo, short of cash and with no cigarettes, was pleased when offered a smoke. Keenly, his friends watched to see if he would take the bait.

He glanced at the hand-rolled cigarette. It looked no different to any other he'd smoked.

'It's okay,' smiled his friend fingering the cigarette. 'Try it. Have you smoked a joint before?'

'Never,' replied Angelo; trying to hide his nervousness. 'I'd rather not.'

'You ****. Take the **** cig,' demanded his friend, egged on by the others.

The badgering grew tense as the language of persuasion changed to aggression and degrading obscenities. He grabbed the cigarette. Raising it to his lips, an array of lighters appeared.

'Take a few drags and hold the smoke for a few seconds and then breathe out,' instructed a mate.

From his first inhalation, the drug seduced him. His mouth and throat felt dry, his heart rate increased and his coordination and balance became impaired. They'd not warned him that smoking cannabis might lead to heightened fantasies, distorted perception and in some instances disturbing reactions, paranoia and hallucinations. Closing his eyes, he felt strong. He lay sunbathing on a beach. A drum banged relentlessly in his head; intensifying with each beat.

'Go on. Suck in and hold your breath.'

He sucked hard and held his breath. Suddenly, the taunting bully laughed loudly and grabbed him in a bear hug. Infused with energy and fearlessness, Angelo threw the man aside. Terrified, the bully shot from the room; trembling. Out of control and oblivious to what was happening, Angelo lifted his heavy metal locker, and with Herculean strength hurled it across the room. Confused and red eyed, involuntary contortions distorted his face. His body performed weird movements. He was gone in mind and body. Now weak and confused, he collapsed on his bed; exhausted. The following morning, his mind blank of events of the previous evening, he woke with a blinding headache. Seeing his belongings scattered around the barrack floor, he knew something drastic had happened. When dragging his locker back to his bedside, the so-called bully kept both silent and his distance. 'What happened?' he asked his mates.

'Not much,' replied one. 'You smoked a joint.'

'I guessed that much.'

Reluctant to tell him, Angelo, during the course of the morning managed to tweeze out the previous night's events from one or the other of them. The bully continued to keep his distance and said nothing.

Later that day, he and his mates strolled through the local park eyeing the talent.

'Here, Angelo, have a joint,' encouraged a mate.

'Not for me, thanks. I had enough last night.'

'It's unpredictable the first time. You'll enjoy this one.'

'Yeah. Go on. Try it, Angelo,' encouraged the others.

He was determined to stand firm. 'I've told you. I don't want any more.'

Keen to watch his reaction when inhaling and have a laugh, the badgering, as experienced the previous night, intensified. Amidst, aggressive enticement and course words, Angelo caved in. 'You'd best sit down for this one.'

Seated on a park bench, he inhaled and held his breath. He felt dizzy. He was back on the beach with the drums beating heavily in his head. His head felt weighty; as if enlarged and too heavy to hold upright; dragging his body down. He came to his senses and stubbed out the cigarette. 'That's enough. No more.' That was the last he touched whilst in the army.

In the disco, the music, the subdued lighting and the free flow of alcohol mingling with the heavy hue of cigarette smoke along with the friendly smiles of encouragement created an ideal seductive atmosphere. The bait cast, resistance collapsed as his friend flicked the spindle of his lighter and grinned widely. Taking the joint, it would not be Angelo's last.

3
An Unnerving Event

Angelo had been in England for almost three months when New Year's Eve arrived. During that time, he smoked cannabis, drank heavily and gambled whenever he could. He was in a nightclub with friends when on the stroke of midnight everyone hugged and kissed one another to welcome in the New Year. A young girl he'd not seen before was standing beside him. Turning towards her, he smiled and then kissed her. Unable to speak English sufficiently to express himself clearly, hand gestures and facial expressions came to his rescue. She took his hand to dance. Following the tense gyrations, and with the help of a few supportive words from friends, he learnt her name was Ann (pseudonym) and fixed a date. From then on, the couple met a few times a week and then the inevitable happened. She invited him to meet her parents.

Not knowing what to expect, Angelo arrived at the house feeling extremely nervous. Despite the language barrier, formal introductions passed smoothly. There were a few tense silences at the dinner table as he patiently waited for his host to serve the meal. He'd never tasted a traditional English dinner. He enjoyed the highly sensitive stimulation to the taste buds by the use of vinegars, oils and cheese washed down with alcohol. In came the gravy bowl followed by a plate of beef and vegetables along with a wafer thin, sky-high, deeply tanned batter balancing on his plate almost obscuring his mashed potatoes. His inquisitive gaze prompted Ann to say, 'It's a Yorkshire Pudding.'

There were a few surprised faces when Angelo politely asked for olive oil and a drink. The visit went well however, and the relationship thrived.

Despite enjoying the company of Ann, his newfound love, the gambling table held its power to lure him into the casino. One particular night, he'd been so intense in placing his bets he'd not swilled down a single pint of beer. He was tired and ready for his nightly fix of cannabis to help him sleep. That was his excuse. In the still hours of that cold January morning he made his way back to the flat above the restaurant with the friend he'd arrived with in England months earlier. An eerie silence shrouded the dimly lit stairway as his pal led the way up to their top floor flat. They'd almost reached the top of the second flight when an icy coldness struck Angelo. He shivered and walked on. The sudden chill intensified. Passing a door, he sensed someone was behind him. He glanced back. A ghostly figure brandishing a long-bladed knife lurched forward to plunge the blade deep into his back. Terrified, he screamed in urgency pushing his friend aside, 'Move! Move! Let me pass!'

'Hey! What do you think you're doing?' snapped his friend, dodging from one side of the steps to the other thinking Angelo was playing games. 'I'll not let you pass.'

'Don't be stupid!' yelled Angelo, pushing him out of the way; desperate to reach his room. Too frightened to look back, believing evil was upon him, he raced up the stairs. Shivering uncontrollably and frantic to escape the situation, on reaching the door, he rammed the key into the lock. 'Come on. Come on. Open!' The hairs on his neck bristled. Urgent seconds grew longer. His hands were icy cold. Suddenly, the door burst open. Into the room he shot. Grabbing the first thing he thought would protect him, he shouted, 'Go away! Go away!' Clutching a crucifix tightly to his chest, breathless and terrified, he jumped fully clothed into bed. Dragging the covers over his head, he longed for whatever had tried to murder him to vanish.

'What's wrong with you?' asked his friend, seeing him cowering beneath the covers. 'You crazy man! You've frightened me!'

Too terrified to move or speak, he hugged the figurine cross; believing it would banish the evil surrounding him. Angelo wished he'd never set foot on England's pleasant land. Desperate to relieve himself, he peeked over the covers for signs of the intruder, 'I need a pee.'

'Go then! I'm not stopping you,' said his friend tucked up in his own bed.

He scanned the room. 'You'll have to go with me.'

'Don't be stupid. I'm not your mama.'

'I'm frightened!'

'Stop being such a pain. You're doing my head in.'

'I'm telling you, I'm frightened.'

'You're mad, man! Come on. Out you get. I'll get no rest until you're settled. I want to sleep tonight.'

Believing he'd die any second, Angelo scurried to the toilet and back, hugging the crucifix.

What he had seen on the stairway had clearly unnerved him. Too frightened to sleep, and still fully clothed, he was thankful when daylight beamed through the skylight. Tired, yet fully aware of his surroundings, he was determined not to spend another night in that place.

Despite his friends' efforts to console him, none could persuade him to stay in the flat. Neither could anyone convince him that perhaps he'd let his imagination run wild. Determined to leave, finding a winter let, he packed his bags and was away within the hour.

That evening at work, gossip of Angelo's ordeal ran wild amongst the staff. Some laughed and agreed he was losing his mind. Others took a more sinister view while some kept silent. A chef said, 'A man died not long ago in the room you passed.'

'What of it?' snapped another, annoyed that he'd told Angelo. 'People die every day. What's so special about that room or that death? Best keep your mouth shut.'

'I'm only repeating what I heard.'

'Shut it, man. Shut it. The hallucination, as many would describe the apparition, could have been drug-induced. You know he smokes cannabis.'

'Think what you want,' said Angelo, 'The fact remains. I saw something sinister that terrified me.'

'Maybe. Who knows?'

'I do.'

Nothing more was said about the incident as each went about their duties.

Only Angelo knew how terrified he'd felt on the stairs. Picking up the crucifix was an act of desperation; a comfort in his hour of need. In his weakened state he'd sought protection in a manufactured symbol of wood and metal that offered no more security than a piece of paper in a raging fire. Fear had been his enemy

- not the unknown. And fear had driven him from his lodgings.

Angelo's second-floor flat was all he desired. He felt safe and settled well in his new surroundings. No more psychic adventures for him! He'd had enough of such things. Making a fresh start, he slept well and felt content. Sadly, he could not forget the fearful ordeal. The trauma had burned deep into his consciousness. He continued to meet with Ann when time permitted, but his love affair with gambling and alcohol continued; as did his nightly smokes of cannabis. During his first days at the second-floor flat, he'd made a new chum in the resident cat. He delighted in stroking its soft brown fur as it purred and rubbed its head and body against his leg whenever it saw him.

Angelo was now sleeping well. As days passed into weeks, his restful nights diminished. No matter how late he went to bed (or early in his case) he woke fearful each morning. He sensed strange things in his room; feelings he could not explain. He'd even been disturbed as early as three a.m. on the days he'd not visited the casino. Unnerved, Angelo moved to the top-floor flat; spending as little time as possible in his new surroundings.

When not working at the restaurant or dating Ann, what spare time remained, he spent at the casino. One night, the gaming had been particularly intense and as usual, when immersed in gambling, not a drop of alcohol had touched Angelo's lips. By three-thirty a.m., he was tired and left alone to walk the short distance to his flat. The streets were silent: not even a sea breeze to kiss the leaves on the tree-lined street as the orange glow of the lamps lit his way. He had almost reached the garden path when a sudden chilled wind whistled around a nearby tree in haunting tones frantically shaking the branches. He felt sick. Goose pimples erupted on his neck. Along the path and into the building he shot. Safely in his flat, he flicked the latch and caught his breath. *I must be going mad. What's wrong with me?* Still trembling, he jumped into bed feeling afraid. Longing for daylight to come, sleep eased his fear. Awakening in daylight, he censured himself for letting a mere breeze and leaves frighten him. Determined to get on with his life, he was soon sleeping well again. One particular morning he awoke full of energy. Shaving in front of his mirror, his door suddenly burst open. In ran the cat with its hair bristling as if electrified. Under his bed it flew. Angelo felt ice cold. Half shaven, he attempted to coax the cat from its hiding place with his hand. 'Out you come.' It hissed; striking out viciously. 'Ouch!' Seeing his hand covered in blood, he shot down the stairs, shaking frantically. 'There's something up there!' he screamed at the proprietor. 'The cat's gone mad. I've had enough of this place. I'm off. You'll not get me up there ever again.'

'Calm yourself, you crazy man. Here, let me see your hand. As I thought. You've been teasing the cat.'

'That's not true. I was trying to lure it from under my bed when it clawed me.'

'Whatever. It's a nasty scratch, but I dare say you'll live. Sit down. I'll bathe your wound and then find the cat. You can finish shaving down here.'

'I'm telling you. There's something up there.'

'Nonsense! Don't be so stupid.'

'I'm not stupid! Something caused that cat to go berserk. Finishing his shave downstairs, Angelo wondered if his friend and the proprietor were right by saying, "You crazy man!" Standing in front of a mirror, fearing he may be losing his sanity, he fixed his eyes on his reflection and cried out in desperation, 'Why me? Why have you let it happen to me? Change me!' Unable to control his fear, he was away within the hour in search of alternative accommodation. Had he known that certain occupants held the belief that the spirits of the dead communicate with the living, he would have avoided the place.

Moving into a fourth flat in another part of the town, he managed to live out the remaining weeks with little disturbance. He knew that things were not right at the various places where he'd lodged. Such was his cumulative fear in the last house, he'd cried from deep within, *Why me? Why have you let it happen to me? Change me!* His cry was a cry for help rather than a questioning phrase. Had he cried, *'Why me, Jesus!'* the tone and inference may well have been one of blame. The sadness of Angelo's plight was that he had no faith. He was an unbeliever - a willing rejecter of God's gift of love.

The winter months were behind him. Time had come to return home. He was glad when Ann decided to go with him. Home would be a welcome haven from the trauma he'd experienced.

Just before leaving for Italy, Angelo heard that a spiritualist had performed an exorcism at the place where he'd had trouble with the cat. Local gossip had it that a spirit of an elderly woman was roaming the house checking that everything was all right. He felt happy when the aeroplane lifted off the runway bound for Italy. He had no plans to return to England.

4
Joy and Heartache

The flight back to Italy passed without incident. He was home and keen to introduce Ann to his parents. He looked forward to an undisturbed night's sleep, the Mediterranean sun and a new life. The pair stayed at his parents' house. For the first few weeks everything seemed fine. While Angelo was on familiar ground, his girlfriend was not. She was homesick. He offered to pay for her fare home, but she relented and stayed. The summer months passed quickly as homesickness raised its head a second time.

Returning to England, they worked the winter months serving at tables and then went back to Italy where Angelo opened a small restaurant. Morning and evening opening times allowed the pair to enjoy the afternoon sun and walk by the sea in the late evenings. These respites brought some benefit, but were only cosmetic. Working in close proximity with one another proved tempestuous. Described as electrifying, Angelo likened the relationship to a negative and positive charge; when touched the inevitable spark exploded. With the relationship under stress, Ann's homesickness increased. Hoping things would improve between them, he sold the restaurant and returned to England. When in Italy, Angelo was free from drugs, but smoked cigarettes. His only gambling activity was to complete the weekly football coupon. He never won.

In England, he worked the first season for others and then saw a coffee bar for sale. His friends advised him not to buy it, saying it would not make a penny.

However, being one who liked a challenge, he bought the place. With lots of hard work, he built the business into a going concern and then sold it. Now married with a son named Rob, he bought a take away business. He also bought a small coffee bar where he taught Ann to prepare Italian style sandwiches and make excellent coffee. She managed the coffee bar and Angelo the business. After building up both businesses, he sold the take away to concentrate on the coffee bar. The business was fine. Sadly, the relationship with the girl he'd kissed on New Year's Eve and married, was under stress. Separation and divorce followed. No explanation is given as to why such a traumatic event occurred. The fact is that two people who had at one time expressed their love for one another had become incompatible.

Unable to work at the coffee shop alongside his ex-wife, soon what money he had, was gone. With a mortgage to pay and limited time to be with his son, Angelo was both broke and broken, and closed to receiving love. The questions he'd asked himself so long ago, *'Why me?'* and *'Change me!'* were far from his thoughts. The world he knew had fallen apart. He took what work he could scrubbing pans, washing dishes and serving at tables. Feeling unloved and rejected, stress overwhelmed him as he slipped without thought of the consequences into a destructive mind set. Believing his life was empty and of no purpose, he cared less about himself and spent what little he earned on alcohol, gambling, drugs and discos. Often drunk, he sank deeper into despair. His health declined as an aura of neglect engulfed him. Projecting a state of unkemptness, his shunning by friends speeded his demise. Apart from trying to take his own life, he did everything he could to destroy himself. As for the things of God, he wanted none of Him. He knew exactly where he stood concerning spiritual interventions. When visitors knocked on his door to explain their particular brand of religion, he screamed, 'Go away! I don't want to know!' Like many who fall on hard times a sudden jolt of reality either pushes the desperate deeper into the mire or lifts them from it. A simple comment related to him by a friend about what someone had said of him, had a profound effect.

'He does not present himself well for business,' were the words. Put bluntly, he looked dirty and like a waster.

Angelo was glad he was sober when hearing the gossip about himself and wondered what path he'd have gone had he been drunk at that time. 'Now I'll show you what I can do,' was his resolve.

He cleaned himself up and worked hard. Within a few months, he'd opened an Italian restaurant with a friend. The restaurant's reputation for good food and fine wine spread far beyond the town; enticing stars from film and television. With business a roaring success, Angelo was in the money. Giorgio Armani shirts adorned his back, and an Alfa Romeo car was his prized possession.

It had been an exceptionally busy evening at the restaurant and after locking up, he and his colleagues headed for the disco. The conversation was friendly and jovial as they walked leisurely along the street.

'Would you like a smoke, Angelo?' asked a friend.

'Yeah.' Believing it to be cannabis, he was surprised when his friend rolled a cigarette incorporating a sprinkle of powder.

'It's much better if you sniff it.'

'Oh. It's that stuff. I'll pass on that one.'

'Don't be so soft. You'll enjoy it.'

'No thanks.'

'Go on,' urged his mates.

'It's nothing much - just a touch of cocaine. Try it. It will give you a good feeling. It's good for your body.' By now, his friend had rolled the fix and lit it. 'Here! Take a drag.'

Not wanting to lose face, Angelo yielded to their taunts and took the joint. Inhaling, his facial expression and raised shoulders projected his deflated expectation.

'Give it a while.'

Having smoked the cigarette, he patiently waiting for the cocaine to take effect. Nothing happened.

'Try another later,' urged his friend.

In business, most people would be thrilled to achieve half of what he had done. But not Angelo. He worked hard at the restaurant and played harder at the casino. He had many friends but remained lonely. Success, money and wanting for nothing did not satisfy his longing. He yearned for something or someone to fill his acute emptiness. He needed a challenge to drag him from his misery. He had everything he ever dreamt of but knew something was missing. He was bored.

Searching for release from his tedium, Angelo bought a small quantity of cocaine and indulged himself. He walked the path which so many hardened addicts take - from tobacco to cannabis to cocaine.

Thankfully, when Angelo inhaled the addictive poison, nothing happened. Had the drug taken hold, who knows what physical and psychological damage it would have caused? Some could say the cocaine he bought was adulterated or even inert powder; hence having no effect. Equally, it could be said that Jesus protected him from the physical and psychological problems which cocaine addiction brings.

Angelo continued his lifestyle much as he'd done prior to opening the restaurant. He thought nothing of drinking four or five bottles of strong beer as well as champagne a day. No matter what comforts he sought, the emptiness he so longed to fill, remained. Such was his heavy drinking it affected his health. He suffered frequent bouts of stomach pain. Abandoning the grade A classified drug, he reflected on his life and directed his energy towards positive activities. *What can I do? What do I know best?* He had only one answer. Turn a failing restaurant into a flourishing concern.

He saw a small coffee shop which was closing down. Again, his friends dissuaded him from buying the property. He and his business partner bought the place and Angelo set about designing the kitchen and customer environment, employing the staff and then building the business. His first restaurant had held a prime position. His new venture was a little way from the town centre and less accessible to casual callers. Working hard to establish the new business, he still managed to drink, gamble and smoke cannabis. When the restaurant became a success, the partnership ended. However, the two remain good friends.

He was intimately involved in drink, drugs and gambling. He'd seen it, done it and had the badge to prove it; so to speak. None of these temporary fixes satisfied him. He remained lost and unhappy.

Angelo's own comments were, 'You certainly know who your friends are when you're down. On looking back, it was as if God's finger was upon me, but I did not know at that time.'

5
A Break in the Darkness

Angelo's restaurant was doing well. He had money to invest and was on the lookout for premises to convert into flats. A hotel came on the market so he arranged a viewing and took a builder to advise him on the suitability of converting the property. He was more than interested when the owner, a broad smiling, brown haired, fast speaking Brazilian woman with wide brown eyes, showed him around. *She's nice*, he thought, hearing her excitable Brazilian voice while watching her gesticulating hands emphasise her words.

The walk around the hotel lasted less than an hour. Angelo was disappointed when the builder announced, 'It's too costly to convert.' Thanking the woman, he left in search of some other property.

Almost a year passed before he met the fiery Brazilian again. He'd helped a friend open a small pizza shop and Anya, his friend's wife knew the woman.

During conversation with the woman, Anya slipped in a casual invitation. 'We ought to go out for a meal, Marina. I know of a lovely restaurant.'

Marina shook her head, 'I'm far too busy to go.'

'But you must. I insist. It's my treat.'

'I don't know if I can.'

'Of course you can. We've not been out together for such a long time. It will do you good.' Fearing Marina might suspect there was more to the invitation than a friendly meal, Anya softened her approach.

Marina's face lit up. 'Okay. I'll go with you.'

The arrangements made and a table booked, off they went to enjoy the delights of Italian cuisine.

Unbeknown to Marina, when Angelo had discovered she was the woman he'd met at the hotel, his scheming mind had rushed into overdrive; persuading Anya to arrange the meeting. Seeing Marina arrive at his restaurant with Anya, his heart rippled with delight. Following formal introductions, Angelo led them to a table. His heart leapt like a schoolchild's when she smiled and said, 'You can call me Marina.'

Suppressing his nervousness and eagerness to impress, Angelo was on his best behaviour; allowing his natural charm and chivalry to overflow. One thought crowded his mind. *Is she married? I hope not!* He would have to work fast if he was to learn more about her. He breathed a sigh of relief when learning she was unattached. Angelo took the drinks order and then departed. His face aglow, soon he was back; spinning the drinks tray high as if undertaking a Royal Variety performance.

The night almost ended in disaster when his nervousness broke through his flamboyant restaurant manner. When pouring her a drink, it ran all over the table, almost drenching his special visitor. Everyone laughed. Too embarrassed to smile, he apologised emphatically for his clumsiness when mopping up the mess. He feared he'd botched his chances to get to know her but he need not have worried, Marina thought him cute. The incident forgotten, Angelo relaxed and was soon cracking jokes and performing magic tricks. By the end of the evening, they'd arranged to meet.

Marina found out afterwards that the meal was Angelo's idea. This did not deter her for by then, the relationship had blossomed. The two were aptly suited; he a drinker, gambler, smoker and drug-taker and she a smoker, tarot card reader and venerator of idolatrous objects. No longer had they to smoke alone. Evening cannabis smokes became the norm.

Determined to succeed in everything she did, Marina sought direction from the numerous gods she worshiped. She kept various idols on a shelf in her flat at her hotel - each defending a different cause. She prayed regularly to them all, lit candles and offered gifts hoping they would shower good favour upon her. Sometimes she prayed hourly to each one in turn. She'd spent a fortune over the years buying packs of tarot cards for varied uses.

The main idols she worshipped were five statuettes made of clay; one of Jesus, one of Mary, one of Saint Expedite (the saint of rapid solutions to problems), one of Saint Germain (the god of freedom and hierarchy for the dawning Golden Age), and one of Buddha. Marina was heavily into New Age teachings and had stacks of books on the subject; along with a heap of Feng Shui literature.

When a particular need arose, she prayed to Saint Expedite for a speedy result. Praying at particular times in the day over a nine-day period, she believed she'd had an answer to her prayers. She was happy. To please the saint, she rang Brazil to order printed cards to give to her friends and tell them of her answered prayer. 'I'll have five hundred cards of Saint Expedite, please.'

'The minimum order is a thousand cards. Do you want to order cards of other saints?' asked the woman.

Marina thought for a moment and then answered with much enthusiasm, 'Yes! Why not? Send me a selection of the others to make up the thousand.' Her credit card details were quickly accepted and she felt happy that Saint Expedite would be pleased with her. Soon, a box of numerous cards arrived from Brazil. With much excitement, ripping open a box, her heart sank. 'Oh no. What can I do with all these? They're printed in Portuguese!'

Unable to hand out cards written in a language that only Portuguese speakers would understand, Marina longed for spiritual comfort.

With Angelo to console her, the disappointment soon passed. She took the hotel off the market and concentrated on building the business. She undertook costly changes to the guesthouse frontage and various improvements to the interior. When finished, everything looked great. She was happier than she'd been for a long time. On receiving a letter from the Town Council, her joy was not to last.

'It has come to our notice that you have undertaken extensive alterations to the exterior of your property without the various planning permissions.

In accordance with our planning regulations, we hereby instruct you to take down such alterations and submit any proposed changes you wish to make to the property for our consideration.'

Deflated, Marina felt it grossly unfair of the council to demand that she dismantle the new frontage. In her naivety, she was unaware that planning permission was required. Not knowing what to do, she put the letter to the back of her mind and continued her daily activities.

One morning, on opening her door, two enthusiastic religious-speaking individuals confronted her. Not wishing to be rude, she listened intently; longing for them to offer some miniscule crumb of hope from which she could take comfort. Not warming to what they said, she stopped their chatter and closed the door. A few days later, two other people stood on her doorstep; expounding their beliefs. Again, she heard nothing to excite her or generate a yearning to rush off to join them. Not long after their visit, an acquaintance of Angelo arrived to speak with him. Angelo escaped to the kitchen, saying he was too busy cooking meals to talk. Marina was also busy, but listened for a few moments to what he said. Later that week, another person knocked on her door to outline the virtues of *her* belief. She had heard enough. Rather than close the door in the woman's face, she let her speak. Thankful to be free of the persistent talker, Marina, in exasperation slammed the door shut.

One mid-afternoon, a couple in their fifties approached the hotel. The man of medium height, stocky build, clean-shaven and with an abundance of white bushy hair, looked a fatherly figure. His face was somewhat reddened and weathered and his hands were worker's hands. The woman who was tall, slim, with short hair and light complexion, had heard that a new place to eat serving Brazilian dishes had opened in the town. Keen to taste the culinary delights, she'd brought her spouse to investigate. On arrival, they were somewhat disappointed to find no such restaurant existed. What faced them was a hotel - one of thousands of such establishments around the town. Reluctant to go home, they rang the doorbell.

'Can I help?' asked a wide-eyed, beaming female.

'We came looking for a Brazilian restaurant and thought it was here,' said the woman.

'No. It's a hotel with a restaurant. You can come in and look around.'

'Are you Brazilian?' asked the man; giving Marina a strong handshake. 'This is my wife, Gill. I'm John.'

'I am. My name is Marina.'

Gill smiled and then spoke in Marina's native tongue - Portuguese.

Marina was thrilled at hearing her native tongue. 'Would you like a coffee or tea?'

'Tea would be nice, thank you,' said John.

As Marina prepared the tea, Gill hoped John would be good. She knew his humour was questionable - not that he embarked on flighty or improper speech. He could be jovial to the point of distraction unless speaking about Jesus. She loved him deeply and delighted in watching his eyes sparkle, his mouth agape, and his shoulders rise and fall when laughing. He, in turn, loved her calm soft melodic voice and took comfort in listening to her play the piano and sing.

'Do you work?' asked Marina as she poured tea.

'I make harps as a hobby. We're retired,' said John.

Gill's eyes sparkled as she looked across at her spouse. 'I've longed to play the harp. They were so expensive so John taught himself and made one for me.'

'That's nice,' smiled Marina.

From first exchanging greetings, a oneness infused the three. Soon they were sipping tea, eating cake and chatting in Portuguese as if best friends.

Marina's eyes widened on learning that John and Gill had been missionaries in Brazil and had lived not far from her town. The pair had not come to preach, but to taste the delights of Portuguese food. In conversation, Gill was sharing how John and she had arrived in Brazil when she quoted a verse from the Bible by way of explanation. 'Jesus said, I am the Way the Truth and the Life. No-one comes to the Father except through me.' Just before leaving, Gill took from her bag a booklet, stuck a sticker on it containing her name, address and telephone number, and then handed it to Marina. 'You must give me a ring sometime and come to tea.' A firm handshake, and the visitors were gone.

What had begun as a social outing for John and Gill had become, on meeting Marina, a time of briefly sharing their faith. In a very natural and spontaneous way, Gill had quoted a verse of Scripture and then handed Marina a simply-worded booklet.

When stepping from the hotel, Gill worried that she'd said too much about Jesus and feared she'd overstayed the hospitality. There in the street, she asked Jesus to forgive her and prayed that Marina would forget any irrelevant words she'd spoken.

Gill need not have worried. Marina had no recollection of any Bible verse, or of Gill mentioning Jesus. The absence of religious connotations had been sufficient stimuli to arouse Marina's curiosity to scan the booklet. The moment her visitors had gone, she deferred the work she must do before her guests arrived and took the booklet upstairs to her flat. Sitting on the edge of her bed, surrounded with her familiar statues, her eyes fixed firmly on the booklet's title, 'Why Jesus?'

The 'Why Jesus?' booklet by Nicky Gumbel outlines who Jesus is, why He came to this earth, died on a cross and rose from the dead. It describes how anyone who accepts Jesus as Saviour can experience His love.

Flicking through the pages, the words *love* and *forgiveness* caught her eye. Turning back to the first page, she began to read. The more she read, the more she could see herself clearly in the pages. She'd read much of the booklet and had come to a part where it asked her to pause and reflect on the things she'd done in her life. Vivid pictures of her past disturbed her. Burdened down by weighty, wearying life experiences, she glanced at the array of statues, tarot cards, bookcases stacked high with idolatrous narrative, candles and the box of Saint Expedite literature. *What am I doing?* Marina experienced a deep void in her life. Decision time was upon her to stay as she was, or to invite Jesus into her life. A talkative, chatty person, now when wanting to say so much, words failed her. She'd been good at praying to the pottery statues, but this was different. Reading the booklet again, she reached the page on which a prayer was printed. *I must pray the prayer.* A short hesitation followed by a deep breath, she spoke aloud as she read, 'Lord Jesus Christ, I'm sorry for the things I've done wrong in my life.' Again she paused to reflect on the life she'd lived. Forceful vivid recollections erupted like a volcano as she realised she was to blame for her hurt as much as those she'd held responsible.

The memories continued for some time; reminding her in colourful imagery of her past. Tears of sorrow at her ill deeds merged with those of repentance when saying, 'Thank you, Jesus that you died on the cross for me, so that I could be forgiven of all my wrongdoings and be set free.'

Not fully understanding the profound change that would take place in her life, Marina spoke aloud her earnest prayer. 'Please come into my life by your Holy Spirit to be with me forever. Thank you, Lord Jesus. Amen.'

The prayer at an end, amidst heartfelt sobbing, she felt her great burden lift and a peace wrap warmly around her; ushering in comfort and assurance. Realising how spiritually blind she'd been in a world of spiritual darkness, she thanked Jesus for loving her and for opening her eyes.

Marina had never experienced what she now felt. She had little insight into the power her prayer had engendered, but knew something very real and special had occurred. She'd asked Jesus to be her friend and knew without doubt, that He loved her. Free from burdens, guilt and shame, she sensed Jesus' Presence; along with an abundance of peace at knowing that He was with her; not only as sovereign Lord, Saviour and King, but also as her very best Friend. Her tears of repentance turned to joy that lasted for hours.

Marina had made a commitment to Jesus. If she would listen, certainly Jesus would direct her path. She was so excited she could not wait to tell the world that she'd asked Jesus into her life. She felt wonderful, happy and blest.

Marina's own comments were, 'Living at the edge is living in darkness. I lived in agony, fear, confusion and sadness. When coming to Jesus, it's like being a new person - a new creation. I don't know how God wants to use me, but I know He has even bigger plans for me in the future.'

Angelo was the first person to see Marina all smiles with face aglow. He could see that something had happened and concluded she wanted something from him.

She'd no idea how to tell him she'd met with Jesus and approached him with caution. 'I think God is calling us to go to church.'

'Us!' gulped Angelo. 'You mean you.'

'No! I don't mean me. I mean us.'

Angelo shrugged his shoulders. 'No way!'

She paused and then with confidence blurted out, 'I met Jesus today. He sent two people who spoke my language.' Marina had caught his attention.

'You must be mad! You're all mad. You're just another crazy woman. If Jesus exists, why does He allow all the hurt in this world?'

'I don't know! Ask Him!'

'No thanks.' Thinking it harmless stuff, Angelo had tolerated her praying to statues but this Jesus thing was a bit too much for him. Gambling, smoking cannabis and drinking six pints of beer a night was enough for him.

Despite Angelo's negative response, Marina knew that Jesus was alive. She had worshipped the various saints that remained on her outside. Now that she had Jesus within her, she was overjoyed. From the moment she had met with Jesus, her daily smoking of cannabis ceased. Prayerfully she questioned, 'What next Jesus?' *To read my Word and seek fellowship with others who love Me* was the answer.

Marina was determined to attend a church. The last time she'd been in one was decades ago; and then only under parental duress. She feared to go alone and longed for Angelo to be with her. She prayed that his heart would soften. However, she knew how determined he was not to attend a place of worship.

6

Two Friends

An unlikely pair to be together, Divine guidance played the major part in orchestrating how John and Gill had met.

When young, John had left England for South Africa with his parents. Gill lived in the south of England. John stayed in South Africa until he was nineteen and then moved with his family to Rhodesia (now Zimbabwe). There he worked as an apprentice diesel fitter. Like many churchgoers who attend church regularly, he believed he was a Christian. One day, while his family was away on holiday, John caught a bout of flu that confined him to bed. The constant long hot days were laborious and tiring for such an active young man. Seeking ways to alleviate his boredom, he picked up a book entitled, 'Basic Christianity' written by John Stott (1921-2011). Flicking through the pages and reading a few paragraphs, he felt urged to read on. Soon, he was well into the book; discovering how Jesus, by dying on a cross, had taken upon Himself all of John's sins, had risen from the dead, ascended into heaven and longed for John to be his friend. He was struck by the sudden realisation that the way he lived his life was not the way he ought to live it. Alone in his bedroom, he invited Jesus into his life and then offered his heart and life to his Saviour. Trusting Jesus implicitly, John decided to live by faith.

When fully recovered, he read his Bible with renewed vigour as the words came alive to him. Reading how John the Baptist had baptised Jesus in the River Jordan, he too wanted to be baptised in water by total immersion. As his church only baptised by the sprinkling of water, he arranged to be baptised at a local Baptist church.

During the last eighteen months of his four-year stay in Rhodesia, he had spent his spare time working at a reformatory for young people. Not knowing where God would take him or what work he would do for Jesus, he agreed to undertake literature work with missionaries in Malawi. God had other plans for him. While lunching with friends, one announced, 'I'm not going to the Missionary Training College in South Africa. I'm considering something else.' On hearing the words, 'Missionary Training College', John knew instantly that God wanted him there. He applied and obtained a place on a three-year missionary training course.

At college, John was the only unattached male. Loved by God, penniless and living by faith, the last thing he wanted to think about was courtship or marriage. He had eyed up a few single women and thought, *What woman would want a man who had no means of providing for her, or had any prospects of doing so in the near future?* As the weeks passed he prayed, 'How will I know whom I shall marry?' He'd started to read the Bible from cover to cover and had reached Genesis chapter twenty-four where Abraham sends his servant to his brother's house to bring back a wife for his son Isaac. The servant arrives outside the city walls and rests at a well. There he prays that the woman to whom he says, 'Please let down your jar that I may drink,' will say, 'Drink, and I'll water your camels too,' will be the woman God had chosen to be Isaac's wife. Soon, a relative of Abraham, named Rebekah arrives to draw water. He says to her, 'Please give me a little water from your jar.'

This she does and draws water for his camels too.

Abraham's servant wonders if she is the one for Isaac. 'Whose daughter are you? Is there room for me and my camels at your father's house?'

Rebekah invites him home where he tells her father that Abraham had sent him, and how he'd prayed at the well. Rebekah agrees to meet Abraham and be Isaac's wife.

Thank you Lord! That's how you're going to do it. John said to himself. The girl who gives me water to drink and invites me home, I'll marry. All John had to do was watch and wait for God to reveal to him the one he would wed.

In his second year at Bible College, the students prayed each Wednesday for missionaries throughout the world. When alone, driving the college's mini bus to take people to the prayer meeting, he heard these words, *John, I want you to go to Latin America.* Rebellious at such clear direction and being more suited to the African environment, he'd not considered that God might take him to another continent. Continuing on his journey the words lingered as his mind raced on. *How can I be sure God spoke to me and what I heard were not self-generated fanciful thoughts?* He wanted confirmation that what he'd heard was from God. Arriving at his first pick up, he prayed, 'If you want me to go there, I want someone to mention Latin America in the prayer meeting tonight.' Unbeknown to John, the prayers at the meeting were to be for African missionaries.

Throughout the prayer meeting, he patiently waited to hear confirmation of the place God would take him. No one mentioned Latin America. John believed the voice he'd heard so plainly had been a passing thought and not a directive from God. The prayer meeting had almost ended when a woman stood up. 'I don't know why I have to read this letter, but I feel compelled to share it with you all. It's from a missionary in Latin America.'

John had his answer. How and when he would go was in God's hands. He was almost at the end of his second year when devastating news hit him. The college would close for good at the end of term.

'What will I do, Jesus? Where will I go?' had been his constant prayer. Not only had he to find another college to complete his final year, he'd be homeless when the academy closed. Devastated, he drew closer to Jesus. Trusting God, he depended totally on Him for all his needs.

At the end of the final meeting which was a farewell service, John still had no place to lay his head. Students had to vacate their rooms, leaving the building empty. Destitute, his prayers unanswered, an elderly woman approached him. 'You can stay at my house if you want. My name is Mrs Field.'

John praised God. His prayer partly answered, he needed to find a place to finish his studies.

When driving him to her house, she said, 'The Lord has told me to pay your fees for the Missionary Training College in Glasgow, Scotland.'

Pleasantly surprised, he thanked Jesus and then his sponsor. *Glasgow! It's a long way from Durban. Why*

Glasgow, Lord? Despite his questioning, he was thrilled that God had answered his prayer. *How am I going to get to Glasgow? I'm penniless, Lord!*

His heavenly Father had everything planned. The church he attended in Durban was building a new extension. Things were tight financially and the congregation was strapped for cash. In obedience to God's direction, the pastor of the church met with John. 'The Lord has told the church to pay for your fare to Glasgow.' Again, he had much to praise and thank God for answered prayer. Off he went to Glasgow Missionary Training College; rejoicing and thanking God that He'd seen and provided for his need.

Gill, when young worshiped at her local Anglican Church. Like John, she'd never questioned her belief until one day at school her teacher asked the class, 'Have we the right to say our religion is the right one?'

A stunned silence filled the classroom, 'No. We do not have the right,' answered Gill with conviction. 'We should be compassionate towards everyone.'

'Had you been a real Christian you would not have said that,' said the teacher.

Those words hit Gill as if struck by a double-edged sword. *Gosh! I do not know what to believe.* Determined to find the answer, she immersed herself in an assortment of books on Christianity including Roman Catholicism. She was still searching for answers when reaching university.

At university, someone invited Gill to the inaugural meeting of the Christian Union. She was not keen to attend, but went out of politeness. Prayer was the theme. Everyone openly prayed except Gill. She didn't know how to pray so decided not to go again - that was until she unwittingly agreed to open the meetings whenever the Union had guest speakers. Whether it was coincidence or God's Word working within her, whenever a visiting speaker came, Gill found herself agreeing to everything he or she said. Not sure what to believe, while eavesdropping on a friend telling someone else about Jesus, things became clear to her. She'd heard her friend quoting Jesus' words from John chapter 16, 'No-one comes to the Father but by Me,' meaning the only way to God is through Jesus. It was as if Jesus had drawn back a curtain and let light into her life. Too frightened to ask others, she'd struggled for years trying to work out 'this religion thing' as she called it. Gill had thought religion was about people respecting God. She was right, but she was searching for more than respecting God. Religion was not what Gill wanted. She desired to know Jesus and have a living relationship with Him. She had many unresolved questions that needed answering and she had not yet fully committed her life to Jesus. A Bible-based preacher came to her church. As he spoke, Gill could not get enough of the gospel.

When visiting a Pentecostal meeting in the town, people started speaking in a strange tongue. She thought they were speaking another language and wanted to run out. 'Oh! I won't go there again,' she told friends.

Opening her Bible, she read how the Holy Spirit fell on those gathered and that they spoke in various languages (Acts 2:1-12). She hadn't read it before and realised that what she'd witnessed at the meeting was the moving of God's Spirit.

She attended a house meeting and continued to visit for over a year. She was hungry for Jesus but still had not made a commitment. She wanted to be sure that her life was heading in the right direction. One evening at the house meeting, a young man read from his Bible, *All of us have become like one who is unclean, and all our righteous acts are like filthy rags; we all shrivel up like a leaf, and like the wind our sins sweep us away,* (Isaiah 64:6). Immediately Gill pictured all her wrongdoing; her sin likened to a piece of toast burnt black. She felt utter despair, but the Lord put into her thoughts a beautiful verse, *'Come now, let us reason together,' says the LORD. 'Though your sins are like scarlet, they shall be as white as snow; though they are red as crimson, they shall be like wool'* (Isaiah 1:18).

For the first time, Gill realised why Jesus had died for her and how He'd personally taken all her wrongdoings upon Himself, forgiven her and washed her clean. This wonderful revelation gave her a real love for the Lord.

While everyone was praying, a woman said, 'God wants each one of us to rededicate our lives to the Lord.'

Gill felt sick. Her mind rushed on. Rededicate my life to the Lord! How can I? I haven't dedicated my life to him once - let alone rededicate it! Gill broke out into a cold sweat and prayed, Lord, I want to give my life to you, but I can't. Can you do something in my life so I can pray that, and really mean it?

Her sincerity was enough. Jesus instantly answered her prayer. There in the quietness of the room, surrounded by likeminded people, she met with Jesus. Every doubt she'd ever had about Him disappeared. She discovered that Jesus was no imaginary figure locked in the depths of her mind but that He is alive! Her head knowledge was now firmly in her heart. She could feel His Presence as He enfolded her in His arms. That day was a turning point in Gill's life - one she'd evaded for so long. Experiencing the touch of Jesus, like John, she gave her heart and life over to His service.

Gill longed to be baptised in the Spirit. Before going to a Bible study about the Holy Spirit, she read from the Bible, *'Therefore, I tell you, whatever you ask for in prayer, believe that you have received it, and it will be yours'* (Mark 11:24).

At the meeting, two men laid hands on her shoulders and prayed. While praying, one man quoted the same words, *'Therefore. I tell you, whatever you ask for in prayer, believe that you have received it, and it will be yours.'* She glowed with an indescribable joy and knew God had filled her with the Holy Spirit.

A few days later, fearful of what would happen, Gill asked the Lord to lead her gently, and that she would trust Him to open her mouth and speak through her in tongues as a prayer language. He graciously answered her prayer.

After leaving university, she studied to qualify as a teacher and undertook teaching practice at a primary school. She needed to find work nearer home so asked Jesus to find her some. Sadly, none was forthcoming.

A Spirit-filled woman said, 'Maybe the Lord wants you to do something else.'

Gill questioned the direction of her life. On reading God's Smuggler by Brother Andrew about him being led by God to a Missionary Training College in Glasgow, she heard God's voice almost audibly saying *This where I want you to go.*

The voice came as a great surprise to her - almost a shock. She knew the voice and what she'd heard was real and not her imagination. She needed God to confirm His direction to her. On viewing a photo of the college, she'd seen the words, 'Have Faith In God' arched over the gateway. She prayed that if this was the place to which God was calling her, those same words would be revealed to her at the evening Bible Study. The words did come up, and three weeks later, the Missionary Training College in Glasgow had accepted her as a student to begin a two-year course.

Gill settled well in Glasgow and studied hard. One particular day it was her turn to read the daily Bible reading. Opening her Bible, she felt somewhat uncomfortable but could not explain why. Regaining her composure, she read aloud how Rebekah gave Abraham's servant water to drink.

John was present. 'Is it her, Lord? If it is, she first has to give me water from a well.'

During the students' free day, Gill had arranged to go walking with friends. John chose to visit a retreat centre at Kilcreggan; a local beauty spot. Gill was ready to leave when rain drenched the land. Abandoning the walk, everyone joined John's group and went to Kilcreggan. At Kilcreggan there used to be three frost-free Victorian water fountains with a water tap plumbed into the side where visitors could draw water. Everyone was sitting at a table talking, when Gill filled a jug from the tap. Pouring the water into a glass, she offered it to John. Believing that this attractive young woman could be the one for him, he took it welcomingly; knowing instinctively, she had to invite him home.

John was in his final year and would be leaving college at the end of term. A few weeks later they were sitting at a table with other students when Gill asked him, 'Where are you going after leaving college?'

'I've arranged to stay with friends in Welwyn Garden City.'

'That's not far from where I live.' Gill wanted to invite John to her parents' house for a meal. Remembering the Bible School Governors discouraged relationships between students, she remained silent. Saddened, she had no peace.

At the end of term when travelling home, she invited John to her parents' house for a meal. Unbeknown to her, John took it as confirmation that they would marry! He suggested God was drawing them together. She said nothing.

A few days later John wrote explaining how God had led him to Glasgow and the confirmation regarding the water and her invitation home.

Gill was utterly perplexed. *If God had shown John so clearly, why had He not shown me?* She would have loved to marry. She had asked the Lord if she would, but as a missionary, she thought she'd probably stay single. *Is this the devil's ploy to divert my thoughts from the Lord?* Her reply to John was swift. *I don't want to hear from you again until the Lord shows me clearly that you are the man for me.*

John never lost hope.

The first weekend of Gill's final year at college was a missionary conference. On hearing a couple who worked in India speak, she questioned, *Perhaps the Lord wants me to go to India. If so, then I'll know that John is not the man for me.* Gill prayed that God would clearly show her through this couple the direction that God wanted her to take. She got a big surprise when the couple spoke about Abraham sending his servant to get a wife for Isaac! Whenever Gill doubted what John had told her, the same passage in Genesis 24 raised its head. Soon she realised that God was drawing John and her together. But where would they go?

John was in London working as a mechanic when, cycling home from church one Sunday evening, a car sped through traffic lights at red. 'Lord, I'm in your hands whatever happens,' he said as the car smashed into him. Hospitalised, he had both arms plastered up to the tips of his fingers and was incapable of doing anything for himself. When sent home, he could not work and had no money. God provided through an anonymous organisation the means to pay his way. Hearing of John's accident, Gill invited him to stay with her family; so confirming the second part of John's conviction.

During the summer months, they prayed together asking God to show them where He would take them. The answer came: *I called on the Lord in distress; The Lord answered me and set me in a broad place* (Psalm 118:5 KJV).

John was working at Mission Headquarters near London. Gill was in Glasgow with weekly calls from a phone box being their only contact. A missionary nurse visited Gill's college and spoke of her work. She was reading the nurse's booklet when her eyes focused on a prayer request for Brazil: *Pray for workers for the vast land of ninety million people.* Sensing that the Lord wanted her there, she asked God for someone to mention Brazil to her on a certain weekend. The weekend came but by ten p.m. on Sunday night, no one had mentioned Brazil. Gill was about to go to bed when a female student walked into her room. 'I've had a fabulous weekend. There was a missionary from Brazil.'

Gill's calling to Brazil confirmed and determined not to influence John, she told no one.

John knew he'd be going to Latin America but had no idea which country. Looking at a map of South America, he sensed Brazil was the place where God would take him. *Wow! Now I know where I'm heading.* Not knowing where God had called Gill, he rang to tell her. She listened and then spoke of how God had shown her the same. They told no one.

Trusting God that He would open the way for them to go to Brazil, John and Gill married. God was faithful and provided the means for them to learn Portuguese and to go to Brazil when the South American Missionary Society offered them paid employment. Much can be said of how God blessed them amid the many hardships, frustrations and joys that they had along the way. Living by faith, they totally depended on God to provide for their needs. Now living in England, they continue to do what God had called them to do - tell of and share with others, Jesus' love.

7

The Past: Forgiven and Forgotten

Until meeting Jesus, Marina's life had been just as turbulent as Angelo's. Despite an active business life, she, like Angelo had experienced emptiness; a void she could not fill. Apart from caring for her children, everything she did had felt meaningless.

Born in Brazil, Marina was the second child of a family of six. Like all concerned parents, her mum and dad ensured she received spiritual guidance by sending her to Sunday worship where confession was obligatory.

Marina's teenage years in South America were chaotic. Parental defiance and an ever-growing rebelliousness simmered deep within her consciousness - awaiting its time to erupt. Like most teenagers feeling their way in a world of experimental youthfulness to things alien to their parents, she was not about to lose face with her friends. Secretly smoking cigarettes stolen from her parents, she'd slip into the bathroom to take a drag. On one such occasion, she was inhaling the smoke when her father knocked on the door. 'Who's in there?'

Up she jumped, desperate to dissipate the smoke and lingering tobacco odour. Stubbing her cigarette out, she flicked it through the open window. 'It's me. I'm in the shower,' she called, frantically turning the shower taps on, undressing, and darting under the spray. Her quick response saved her that day. Her source of tobacco dried up when her mother stopped smoking. By then Marina was using drugs and moving in unsavoury circles. Despite her rebellious behaviour, she managed to keep her misconduct well hidden from her parents.

To them and to the rest of the community, she projected an image of a responsible angelic girl. Only her friends saw her wilfulness. Accepting her bad behaviour, she lacked the willpower to halt the decline in her waywardness.

Forgetful to dispose of a joint of cannabis she'd been smoking when out with her mates, her mother, when cleaning Marina's room, found it tucked away in a matchbox. Confession time did not spare the rod. Warning her of the dangers such illicit activities bring, her mother beat her severely. Caught, warned and punished, the words and beating served only to feed defiance as her clandestine activities deepened.

Tragedy struck the family when Marina's dad died suddenly. She was seventeen. A year later, she moved into a flat with two female friends to allegedly study at a college. Working in a shop throughout the day and attending to studies in the evenings, education was not the driving force in her life. The freedom to do what she wanted whenever she liked, appealed to her. Out dancing every night until the early hours, drinking alcohol, smoking tobacco and cannabis became her lifestyle.

Working hard during the day and playing harder at night took its toll. One particular day she arrived at her flat to find a party in full swing. Too exhausted to take part in the drinking, drugs and the demands of the boys, she hid in her bedroom until her roommates dragged her out calling her names and saying she was no longer one of them. From there on arguments broke out. Resisting their chants of rejection, she wanted to leave but had nowhere to go. The cannabis her friends basked in had moved up a notch to the more dangerous substance of cocaine. The side effects of both drugs were destroying her friends. She'd been a willing participant in smoking, drinking and drug taking, but drew the line when her friends wanted her to inject heroin. An accumulation of late nights, early mornings, dancing, drinking and hard drugs were causing her friends to have mood swings. Their hallucinations and mounting social problems unnerved Marina to the extent that she felt unsafe. Seeking to escape from the scene, a young man took her to a hostel for females run by nuns. Meantime, the facade of innocence continued when ringing home. She stayed at her boyfriend's house more than at the refuge.

Eventually she moved away, took a job as a trainee tourist guide and learnt as much as she could about the local area. Portuguese, her native tongue, was no problem - neither the smattering of Spanish she knew. Speaking English was difficult. She'd learnt a little at school, but found conversational English different from anything she'd previously encountered. Her tourist guide ambitions did not last. Soon she was jobless.

Her dad had wisely invested money for her, and on his death, she was free to spend it on whatever she wished. Keen to make a success of retail marketing, she bought a few cans of oil, sold them, bought more, sold them, until she'd built up a large enough stock to fill a shop from floor to ceiling. Living near the borders of two adjoining countries, she had only to cross a bridge to reach either. Soon she had a thriving distribution network. Oil bought at home and taken across the border where engine oil cost a higher price, seemed a logical business venture. There was a snag in the shape of export law, customs officials, border control and the police.

The first trip across the border was the most fearful and daring. Driving her car loaded with cans of oil plus a pocket full of cash to slip to the border guards, she was on her way. The few minutes crossing the border which was a bridge with checkpoints at each end, seemed endless. Checked at both ends, guards waved her through. It seemed all too easy. The crossing successful and the transaction done, she was keen to cross more frequently.

The business was booming when she met and fell in love with an honest young man. He played no part in Marina's business venture and knew nothing of her dealings - especially with the police. The business continued to grow, as did the bribes. Everyone got his or her share. Soon she'd enough cash to rent a shop as a base across the border.

Each trip became a way of life; stock up, pay out, cross the bridge, sell, return and repeat. She even had an admirer in one of the border guards. In hope of a permanent relationship, the officer let her enter the country without taking his backhander. He knew she had a boyfriend, but didn't care. Things got out of hand when he wanted a strong physical relationship rather than a platonic friendship.

The shop across the border was vulnerable to thieves and police harassment. She had her eye on a shop on the Brazilian side - a prime site from which to generate a good income. Closing the shop across the border, she rented one in Brazil. The building took every reais [pound] she had. With no cash to buy goods and bare shelves, it was not such a promising start for a budding entrepreneur. Determined and ambitious, within a year the shop was full of stock including refrigerated drinks. Her main buyers were fifty youths who walked the streets carrying iceboxes selling to the locals and tourists waiting to cross the border. Her business and long-term relationship with her boyfriend was going so well that marriage was becoming a possibility.

She had spent a few days with her mum who lived ten miles away and returned home earlier than expected. Dumping her suitcase in the hallway of her bungalow, she was thrilled to be home and longed to feel her boyfriend's loving arms around her. Suddenly she heard noises coming from her bedroom. *Burglars!* Her heart pounded. Foolhardily, she approached the bedroom. Flinging the door back, her eyes widened and her temper flared on seeing the man she loved in bed with a woman. Shocked, angered and hurt, numbness gripped her. Grabbing her suitcase, she hurried away. The relationship with the man of her dreams was over. Up until that time, she'd commanded every situation. Believing she could control all men proved to be an illusion. Deeply hurt, she felt betrayed and destroyed to the extent that she would never again trust a man. Distraught and heartbroken, she dragged her suitcase to the nearest estate agent and leased a bedsit. Alone in unfamiliar surroundings, her pent up emotions exploded mightily with tears of sorrow, anguish and pain until no more tears could flow.

As the weeks slipped by, strange things began to happen. A dead frog lay near her door. Placed in

Marina's direct path where she could not fail to see it, hung a dead chicken, arranged to send a firm message from a tormentor. Distressed and fearful, the taunts continued. Not knowing what to do, she approached a friend.

'You need a soothsayer, a fortune-teller or an occultist,' advised her friend. 'You must defend yourself at all costs. It's the macumba [black magic]. Someone is trying to kill you.'

She'd caught her boyfriend in bed with a woman, had left him, had his baby, was weak and stressed, her mind burning with hurt, and now this. Not thinking logically, Marina wanted to smash the one who'd caused her such pain. She had a fair idea of who had deposited the frog and chicken but had no proof.

'If you want to protect yourself, you must defend yourself,' insisted her friend.

In her helpless state, seeds of revenge mushroomed into vengeance equal to that of her tormentors. Knowing no other way to protect herself from the Black Magic, she directed her hate towards her ex-boyfriend. Taking her friend's advice and in her vulnerability, she sought the help of a practising occultist.

Out came the tarot cards; opening the way to a divisive manipulation. The reading was not good. Battle lines were drawn and the vengeance prescribed. The ever-increasing price of the occultist services was £30. The cost to Marina in heartache, pain and distress was immeasurable psychological agony.

The taunting continued. Further visits followed. 'We must take drastic measures to stop the attacks,' advised the occultist. 'You'll need me to sacrifice a chicken,' adding, 'It will cost you a bit more. Have you the cash?' Assured that the killing of a chicken was the only way to obtain a victorious outcome, she was desperate and paid readily. The sacrifice did not quell the fearful psychological trauma.

As the months rolled by, Marina met a business acquaintance who sold cigarettes. He was short of cash and asked her to fulfil an order. This she did. Little did she know how the business would grow. Starting small, she bought job lots of cigarettes at a very reasonable price and sold them at a profit. The cigarette business took her away from the drinks trade, so a female friend named Dene managed the wide distribution network of fresh fruit drinks, beer and carbonised drinks. The cigarette business grew so fast she had money to spare so bought a house to store the stock.

During this busy time of buying, selling and seeking her revenge, an associate had stock he thought Marina might buy. Insisting that she meet with him, he arranged a venue to negotiate a price and clinch the deal. At the last minute, she could not go so Dene and her boyfriend Antonio went to the rendezvous in Marina's four-wheeled vehicle. On parking beside a market stall, four men jumped into the car. The pair shook in terror when one pushed a gun into Antonio's ribs. 'Drive!' he said threateningly.

Directed by the man, Antonio drove at high speed to a lonely spot far out of town. There was no mercy shown as the gunman menacingly waved his gun at the pair as his henchmen dragged them from the vehicle. 'Where is it?'

'Where's what?' asked, Dene, terrified as to what the men wanted, and more so as to what they might do.

'Don't mess with me,' snapped the assailant striking Dene across her face. 'The money! Where's the cash?'

'We have no money!' yelled Antonio.

A quick nod to his mates, the leader watched as they beat the youth unmercifully. Onto the ground he fell. Wriggling and screaming in agony, heavy boots pummelled him.

'Stop it! You're killing him!' screamed Dene, trying desperately to pull the men away from her boyfriend. Not strong enough to stop them, the attackers threw her to the ground.

'Enough,' said the leader. 'It's in the car.'

Leaving the girl to comfort her boyfriend, the kidnappers ripped out the car's seats, carpets, door panelling and anything removable in search of cash. Finding none, the leader pointed his gun at the anxious pair. 'Go! If you as much as breathe a word to anyone or look back, we'll kill you.'

Too hurt to run and thankful to be alive, they scurried away as best they could. They'd not walked far when the roar of the engine, the cranking of the gearbox and the sound of screeching tyres broke the silence as the assailants fled the scene leaving their victims to bake beneath the hot Brazilian sun. Frightened and distraught, the two struggled home. A few days later, the police found the car abandoned.

'They wanted you, Marina,' said Dene.

'It seems that way,' replied Marina with concern for Dene's safety more than her own. 'We'll have to be careful.'

Although she had all she desired in plenty of cash, she still felt unloved and grossly unhappy. Her business domain was strong. As the cash rolled in, others cast their eye on her success. In the dead of night, wagon after wagon slipped into the driveway of the house. Not a single cigarette remained as thieves systematically stripped her store of its merchandise. The goods gone, and unable to seek legal redress by informing the police, Marina was devastated. She'd had enough. What with the border guard pestering her for sexual favours, her troubles with her ex-boyfriend and the kidnapping of Dene along with the theft of her stock, she decided she truly had had enough. She sold up and bought a shop in the town centre selling books.

The longing to exact revenge on her ex-boyfriend while protecting herself from the unwanted attacks on her mind, gave her no peace. Unable to find rest and harmony in her life, she met with various people who used tarot cards, held precious stones and used pyramid structures in their worship of many gods. Fascinated by what they believed and by the way they lived, she became involved and stocked her bookshop with literature on spiritual healing and the using of precious stones, charms and pyramidal structures. To attract buyers into her shop, she had a pyramid in which customers could sit and meditate.

Cramming her life with everything she thought meaningful, the huge void she'd tried to fill opened wider. Sadly, the taunting and cycle of fear did not stop as each occultist's consultation cost ever-increasing amounts of money. As each attempt to be free from further taunts failed, action, which was more drastic, followed as each practitioner passed her onto someone more experienced in black art.

'The root cause of your trouble is that you have a knot in your life that must be untangled before moving on,' warned one practitioner. 'Do you want to unravel the knot or be bound forever by this evil?'

'I have no choice but to seek release,' said Marina. 'What else can I do? No matter what the cost, I must free myself and my family from these attacks.'

'Then you must appease the spirits if you are to be free.'

Her fear had moved from an initial visual encounter with a frog and chicken to a threat from an unseen force. Advised to please the spirits, the instructions on how and when quickly followed along with the obligatory demand for larger amounts of cash.

'Twelve midnight is the time. The graveyard is the place,' said the practitioner.

The advice given and the money paid, she saw no other way by which she could avenge her hurt and stop the harassment.

Marina shivered uncontrollably when gathering the prescribed food offering. By nightfall, everything was ready. Convinced she'd never again have to do such harrowing actions, she sat nervously waiting for the time to leave. Her only consolation, no matter how misguided, was the thought of being free from further taunts. At a quarter to midnight, she tucked her bag of gifts beneath her arm and cautiously stepped into the night air. A night of full moon, fearing someone might see her, she edged her way along the silent streets, determined to conquer her foes. On entering the graveyard, she hyped her vengeance by focusing on her hurt.

Where is it? she questioned ferreting through the graves in search of a specific gravestone. *I'll never find it. Everything looks so different at night.* Her anxiety and fear heightened as the prospects of not finding the right grave intensified. Panic was about to erupt when her hand touched the headstone. Hastily placing her offering on to the grave, she fled the scene, thankful that her ordeal was over. Safely home, she breathed deeply and sank into her chair, believing everything would be fine.

Her life muddled, confused and deeply troubled, love blossomed when she met her ideal man who was a highly respected business entrepreneur. Eight months after finding her partner in bed with a woman, Marina married the mogul. She had everything in life; a man who doted on her, a father for her son, a large four-bedroomed flat, a swimming pool and servants to pander to her every need.

Although her husband truly loved her and did everything he could to please her, she was not content and sensed there was something missing in her life. Like fungi silently smothering every cell in her body, the deep hurt she felt concerning her ex-partner's actions continued to fester. The love her spouse showered on her was unrequited. A fiercely independent woman, her marriage was doomed from the outset.

Restless, as if struggling to break out of an invisible cage, her free spirit took her from Brazil to Spain. In Spain, she met a highly intelligent Englishman. The relationship blossomed, but her few months of happiness quickly passed. Returning to Brazil, she knew her marriage to the loving man was over. Separation and divorce quickly followed.

Heading back to Spain, Marina's relationship with the Englishman deepened. Marriage in England followed. She was happy and returned to Spain with her new spouse. The taunts behind her, the visits to the occultists and the graveyard encounter suppressed deep in the depths of her mind, she felt happy and content that she'd found love.

Life was good in Spain. She hoped her time there would never end. Hating the times when her spouse took business trips home to England, she really missed him and longed for his return.

Their time in Spain ended and the three journeyed to England. She knew only a little English and felt apprehensive. However, Marina decided to make the best of what she had and attended a college to learn the language. As her English improved, she worked early mornings and evenings as a care assistant. Between shifts, she studied anatomy, reflexology, aromatherapy and sport massage related to stress injuries. Despite her enthusiasm for the subjects, business was her forte. Considering numerous business opportunities, she and her spouse bought a hotel. Sadly, on arriving at the new place, their relationship ended. Divorce followed.

8
Real or Just a Fad

Since meeting with Jesus, Marina was determined to attend a church but feared what type of reception she might receive. Angelo had refused to take her. Plucking up courage, she picked her moment and asked him again. 'I'm going to church. Come with me.'

'Me! You must be joking! I've told you once. I'll not go. You go if you want, but I'm not.' He'd no interest in going to any church. His vision of such places remained polluted by childhood memories. He'd had enough of religion and wanted no part of it. To him, churches were like a club for gangsters who hand out a weekly blessing in exchange for cash.

Marina was desperate to find a church where she could worship and share fellowship with those who love Jesus. 'Please come with me.' She hoped her pleading was enough to break Angelo's determination not to go.

Oh, go with the woman. Anything to stop her nattering was Angelo's silent response. 'All right. All right! Stop nagging! I'll go with you.'

Marina was happy and relieved. As the day drew near, her expectations of enjoying wholesome fellowship heightened. She hoped to find a church where she could freely worship Jesus from her heart. A post-reformation church was her choice. When she entered the building, powerful images came to mind of the church opposite the one she'd attended back home. The warning, cemented firmly in her psyche when young, screamed in her head, *Never set foot in that church!*

It's the work of the devil! So strong was the warning she was fearful of entering. Those childhood commands given by the family patriarch remained powerfully controlling. *Dare I?* A battle raged within her. *Am I to obey or disobey family instructions?* She'd disobeyed family directives before, but this was different. *I'm no child. I have the power to decide what and what not to do.* Trusting Jesus, bravely she entered the church. The congregation sang a few hymns and then listened to the sermon. Well, Marina did! Angelo switched off his brain, closed his eyes and slept. There were many elderly people and a few young ones present. After the service, everyone was kind and most welcoming. They even offered the visitors coffee. Angelo let Marina do the talking. She left happier than when she'd arrived, but did not feel comfortable. He was glad Marina had rejected it. The seats were too hard for sleeping on and the coffee was not to his liking.

Amidst her disappointment, she knew Jesus was calling her to a place of worship but didn't know which one. 'Surely there is some church I can go to, Jesus?' Confident she'd receive an answer, and desperate to have fellowship with other believers,' she said to Angelo. 'I really feel that we should return to the church we know best.' Hoping she'd change her mind, Angelo said nothing. Sunday arrived. Marina remained enthusiastic and dragged Angelo to the nearest pre-reformation church where ritual reigned.

On the church steps, he entered believing that Marina's change of heart was just a whimsical fad and would soon pass. When he saw the confession box, he sniggered. He'd confessed to a few small wrongs when young and kept quiet about the big ones. He'd learnt early in life that the more he confessed, the bigger penitence he had to do. More worshippers arrived. His eyes fell on a crucifix. His sniggers changed to fear when picturing how he'd formerly clung to such an object in frightened rage. As the smallest of reminders triggers pleasant and unpleasant memories, the awakening of such events often results in devastating consequences. The simple act of lighting candles and the dropping of coins in a nearby box made Angelo uncomfortable. Suppressing such recollections, he was pleased when the hymn singing started; allowing plenty of time to sleep. Making himself comfortable in the pew, he shut out the noise and dozed. Past events pestered him. He was in Italy reliving the trauma of adjusting to civilian life after National Service. His dreaming carried him to a local coffee bar; jobless and sitting with two unemployed school pals. The futility of having no money and the endless hours of boredom washed over him. He recalled how the three had lived meaningless lives while watching others prosper. He sensed the hopelessness of the situation and their twisted view on life. Seeking to break the monotony, a pal said, 'I bet you can't smash a few car windows.'

Angelo felt brave. 'Try me.'

'Come on then. Let's see what you're made of.'

Off they went down a quiet back street to test Angelo's nerves. There was no way he could back down now.

Passing a car, his friend spied a coat on the back seat. 'Nick it if you dare.'

'Watch out for me while I grab it.' Angelo looked around to see if anyone was watching him. Taking a loose stone from a wall, he smashed the car window, grabbed the coat and was away before his mates realised he'd done the deed. Winning the bet, he proved he was as fearless as they were. From then on, his friends encouraged him to do acts that were more daring. He likened the dares to a school. The lessons started simply and then got harder until the ultimate test of the examination.

Angelo and his friends felt no pain and laughed heartily on completing each test. Never once did they consider the hurt and anxiety caused to their victims. Smashing car windows and stealing worthless items was part of their game. None needed or wanted anything they stole. On many occasions, they simply threw away what they'd taken. The thrill and excitement rather than the dare, drove them on - a thread that ran throughout Angelo's turbulent life.

Tired of petty thievery, their daring became more sinister. A test of obedience, an initiation into the darker world, or just a step too far and Angelo was heading for prison. He lived life as if he were an apprentice lawbreaker. The more examinations he passed, the nearer he came to his degree as a fully-fledged professional criminal. He was not ready to collect his diploma. He failed to realise he was being groomed for gangland. Law breaking had become a habit - a way to get his daily adrenaline fix.

Setting a dare, his friends assured him they would be with him. Nearby stood a church wrapped in scaffolding while undergoing restoration. Just beyond the doorway stood a table on which lay candles and a large wooden collection box. Those who wished to light a candle were welcome to buy one, light it, and then pray for something or someone.

Angelo with one other entered the church, while the third kept watch. His friend stopped at the inner door, urging him on. Lifting the coin box, he hid behind one of the many church columns. Joined by his friend, the two tried to open the box with a screwdriver. Neither realised that the simplest sound echoed around the building; alerting inquisitive folks. Soon the distinctive sound of a police siren filled the air.

'The cops are here!' screamed his friend. 'Run, Angelo! Run!' Seeing the police dashing up the church steps, his friend bolted while the other scrambled up the scaffolding.

As if experiencing a catatonic episode, Angelo could not move. Petrified, his fingers clasped the box. He trembled. *Why am I doing this? I must be mad to be stealing from a church.* He pictured himself in the dock waiting for the judge to pronounce sentence. *What will mum and dad think of me? I've shamed them.* For the first time in years, he felt guilty. Suddenly, a strong arm of the law grabbed him.

'You're under arrest,' said the police officer; showing no mercy when dragging him to the awaiting police car. Hit, punched and kicked, and now bent low with the force of the police arm lock, he could see the priest smiling and nodding in satisfaction. He received no protection from the excessive force by those professing to forgive sins. Yes, he'd done wrong, but his actions did not give those custodians of the law the right to indulge themselves in violence. Caught in the act, Angelo had no defence or offenders' protection. His friends did not escape either.

At the police station, the two officers threw him into a cell and again punched, kicked and slapped him before questioning for many hours. Pressurised to admit to crimes he'd not committed, he refused. Left to stew, he had time to think. Aware of his weak position, he decided enough was enough. He knew his next test was to commit a much more serious criminal offence whereby someone would be injured or even killed. Following a firm warning from the custody sergeant, Angelo had yet to face his father. Neither the police nor the church brought charges against him or his friends. Many hours passed before the police called his mother to take him home. How he'd escaped a jail sentence, he did not know. His dad said nothing. His fearsome glare and the message written clearly on his face were stronger than words could express. *Do anything like that again and I'll kill you myself.*

Glad to be free, the fumbled crime was a warning. A renegade without a job, prospects or qualifications, he knew something terrible would happen one day. He felt guilty and ashamed that he'd stolen from a church. Something had stirred within him. He quit the gang and walked a different road - a straighter path, but not the one he would eventually walk. That road was a long way ahead. Determined to reform, he recalled the various jobs he'd done as a labourer, car attendant, builder and plumber. None had been right for him. Cooking and restaurant work was what he knew and so he returned to work with his dad.

Angelo's recollections of past events abruptly ended. 'Ouch! My leg hurts,' he complained as cramp dragged him back to reality. He wanted to leave the church immediately. He glanced at Marina. She too felt uncomfortable.

She had been sitting next to an elderly male who glared suspiciously at her; void of a welcoming word or a smile. When the singing started, Marina had no hymnbook. She'd tentatively glanced at the one the man held. He was not impressed. He shuffled his feet, glared at her disagreeably and then turned away taking his book with him.

That's a nice welcome. I thought everyone should be nice to each other, thought Marina. She'd sung the hymns, and felt nothing. She longed to sing from her heart - not her head. When the singing had ended, everyone sat to listen to the priest. Like Angelo's, her thoughts had wandered. She recalled the days of her youth. She pictured the times her parents had made her attend church and sit like a dummy too frightened to move. With each utterance of the priest, she knew what came next. Although the service was in English, the content was the same. Nothing had changed. The church of her youth, the one she knew most, was not for her. This was not what she'd pictured. No sooner had the service ended and the pair were out in the street.

Not willing to accept defeat, Marina kept hope alive, while Angelo wondered how many more gruelling memories he must endure before she rejected her cause.

Marina remembered she had Gill's phone number. The preliminaries were short. 'I've read the book and said the prayer. Do you mind if I go to your church? I'll come this Sunday. Is that okay?'

Gill was thrilled to hear that Marina had met with Jesus. 'Of course you can. I'll wait for you at the church doorway. The service starts at ten thirty.'

She could not wait to tell Angelo. 'I'm going to church this Sunday. Will you go with me?'

'Not again, woman. I've taken you to two services and that's enough for me. If I'm to go anywhere, it's to the betting shop.' This time he was adamant.

Sunday came and Marina set off for Gill's church with Angelo trailing behind her; his reluctance projected on his face. On approaching the church steps, Marina spied Gill with outstretched arms and a beaming smile. By the time she had reached the church door, Gill had given her a big hug. Comforted by the welcome, Marina returned the love showered on her.

Angelo did not share their enthusiasm. Harbouring much suspicion, he followed her into the building, wondering why he had ever agreed to go with her.

A short grey haired woman of about seventy, her face glowing with a warm smile and kindly eyes, shook his hand. 'It's lovely to see you,' she said in a soft Scottish accent. 'Would you like a newsletter?'

Not knowing what a newsletter was, he took it and trotted after Marina much like a reluctant child being dragged to a new school. Once inside, he flopped onto the back central pew; determined to pick fault at everything he saw.

Marina, not knowing what to expect, sat beside Angelo; more ready to accept the situation as the congregation milled around chatting and greeting one another.

To the left near the front of the church, a number of people were tuning their guitars, adjusting the microphones and generally preparing to lead worship.

Angelo glanced their way. He was not impressed. It's a bit of a crazy place. What's all this disco?

Soon the church was bustling with people of all ages. The *disco*, as Angelo had named it, played tunes he'd never heard before. Everyone stood to sing, clap and sway to the music. Some even raised their hands.

These people are mad. What's all this lifting of hands? Why am I here?

The worship group, a small assembly of pianist, drummer, bass guitarist, mandolinist, flautist and three singers had set the tone of the service by playing and singing a number of praise songs joined by the congregation. The raising of hands was later explained to be a natural outward expression of love, joy and oneness with their Lord and Saviour Jesus Christ.

Angelo was tired. He'd worked late at his restaurant and had been up early cooking breakfast at Marina's hotel. The cannabis he'd smoked and the beers he'd drunk the previous evening had not had the desired affect he'd hoped for - in fact, quite the opposite. He had a lousy headache and his stomach ached. Loud music, no matter how melodically played and lots of folk singing their hearts out, clapping and raising their hands, was the last thing he wanted to see or hear. His patience reached breaking point when someone passed a green cloth bag along the rows of people as each in turn dropped notes and coins into it. He grumbled as the collection bag passed by. *Why should I give anything to these people? They should get out and work for a living, as I do.*

By the time the pastor rose to speak, Angelo had had enough. He closed his eyes and fell asleep. The service had ended when Marina nudged him. She'd been suitably impressed with the whole event and wanted to return the following week. Such was her excitement at knowing Jesus, she told everyone about what He had done for her. Knowing and experiencing God's love, she knew that Jesus was alive and loved her. She looked forward to attending church regularly and hoped that Angelo would understand and continue to go with her. She felt happy, until an envelope fell through her letterbox.

Like most who wish their troubles would vanish, she'd tried hard to forget the little matter of planning regulations. Not hearing from the council for months, she'd assumed they had somehow dropped the matter. Breaking the seal, her heart sank when reading the content. *No! It's not right. Surely, there must be some mistake. Impossible!* There was no mistake. The wording was very clear. The new frontage she'd fixed to the hotel and paid so much for was in breach of planning regulations and had to come down. This was her final notice. If by a particular date she'd not removed the new façade, the council would start court proceedings. *It's so unfair!* Her heart raced and her stomach churned when picturing the men dismantling the elaborate signage. *Why now?* she questioned. *Why now? I was so happy.* Distraught and feeling low, she cried aloud to Jesus. Thinking of ignoring the letter, somewhere deep in her heart she knew she must conform to the law. She sought John's advice.

He was in no doubt as to what she must do. 'Those who love Jesus must obey the law of the land.'

Marina obtained a number of quotes for the work to be carried out. It had been such a costly mistake; not made to create confrontation, but to enhance the appearance of the building. Despite the final notice, she decided to do nothing until the letter from the court arrived. She had told Jesus about her concerns a number of times and even cried out for Him to help her. Trusting Jesus, Marina returned to church and enjoyed the fellowship. Angelo went too, but slept throughout the service. He looked forward to his forty winks there. A few months passed, and much to his surprise, Marina was still praising Jesus.

The date for the removal of the frontage came and passed - then the dreaded letter arrived. The day of reckoning had come. With trembling fingers, Marina fumbled to open the envelope not daring to think what it would say. She hesitated, breathed deeply and pulled out the letter. Opening it, her eyes fixed on two words - *case dismissed*. She could hardly believe her eyes. 'Thank you, Jesus! Thank you, Jesus!' she shouted, her face aglow and clutching the letter to her breast. 'Truly you answered my prayer.' To Marina, her answered prayer was her second miracle - the first being, she'd met with Jesus. Jesus had not forced himself into her life, rather the opposite: she'd asked Him.

There were many more answers to prayer relating to day-to-day events. One Bank Holiday morning, the hotel's electricity suddenly failed at eight thirty in the morning. The place buzzed with guests and tempers flared when they tried to run baths, dry hair or make drinks. Marina called her electrician. Soon all would be well.

After many hours of searching, the artisan shook his head. 'I've tried everything but can't find the fault. I've no idea what's gone wrong.'

By mid-afternoon, the guests were irate. Some threatened to leave. Around 5 p.m. the electrical problem remained a mystery. 'I'll have to start taking up the floorboards,' announced the electrician, shaking his head as they stood in one of the rooms.

Marina was desperate. She knew enough to know that the devil was keen to destroy her blossoming relationship with Jesus. She also knew Jesus had promised that in her weakness He would make her strong. Holding on to that promise, she cried out aloud to Jesus asking Him to hear her prayer and make the electricity flow. Much to the electrician's surprise, she had hardly finished praying when the television burst into life and the lights glowed brightly. 'Thank you, Jesus! Thank you, Jesus! Precious Saviour! Thank you Jesus!' was her cry.

On another occasion, when the printer stopped functioning, a prayer had it working in no time. Some may say that such things are coincidence, but those who put their faith in Jesus know otherwise.

Marina had never read a Bible. Now that Jesus was real to her, she yearned to know Him more, and asked Gill to help her understand God's Word.

Without being pushy, demanding or overbearing, Gill lovingly guided Marina through the New

Testament; explaining and encouraging her to take nothing for granted, but to let Jesus speak to her through His Word. With Jesus as her Guide, her desire to know more of Him became a hunger for God's Word.

'Not that again,' said Angelo, seeing Marina pick up her Bible. 'It's not true.'

'Think what you like. I know it to be otherwise. This Bible is God's written Word. It tells of His dealings with human kind, especially with you and me. It's a love story from beginning to end; a book you should not neglect.'

'Don't get so touchy.'

'If you read it, you might realise there's more to life than going to the betting shop.'

Angelo shrugged his shoulders. 'I hear there are too many *thees* and *thous*.'

'That's no excuse. You could read an Italian Bible or the New King James Version.' Marina thought she was getting through to him. She was sadly mistaken.

'You read what you want, but stop pestering me. I'm happy the way I am.'

His resistance to the things of God did not stop Marina from encouraging him to read a few pages whenever the topic arose. He never did. She wanted to be like Jesus and did everything she could with love and compassion in her heart. When studying her Bible with Gill, she would rush home to share her learning with Angelo - that's if he would listen. 'I want people to see Jesus' love in me,' she told him. 'I want them to sense my joy at knowing Jesus and feel the peace He gives me.

I want patience, kindness and goodness to be part of my character.'

'Patience is a hard request. You're forever rushing from one thing to another.'

'You know what I mean. I want to show patience and tolerance to others and be forgiving.' Above all else, I want to be faithful to Jesus.

He knew what she meant. Since the day she'd met Jesus, he'd seen a change in her. 'Sounds good to me. I look forward to seeing you more loving, happier and peaceful - especially being more tolerant and forgiving towards me.

'It's no joke.'

Angelo accepted that improving relationships with others was a good idea, but to attempt the impossible may well prove difficult.

As the days slipped by, Marina tried her best to be all that she'd said. Since reading her Bible, she wanted God's Spirit to dwell in her, but first she had issues in her life she wanted to resolve. Even though she knew Jesus was with her, the statues, tarot cards, New Age books and the Saint Expedite cards continued to occupy their space, if not her time. Whenever she looked at them, she felt a heaviness of heart and decided to get rid of them: the problem was, how? She contacted Gill for advice. 'I think the Lord is telling me to throw out all the paraphernalia I have in my flat. The problem is, I don't know what to do with it. If I take it to the tip it might fall into the wrong hands.'

'You could burn it,' replied Gill.

'How? It will take me years to burn it all at my place.'

'Bring everything here. We'll burn it in the field.'

Marina thanked Jesus for laying it on her heart to rid herself of all the idols, tarot cards and literature, and for providing the solution. After taking down the statues and removing the box of answered prayer cards from Brazil along with the numerous packs of tarot cards, she felt at peace. There were stacks of the stuff. She filled several large black bin liners with books on the occult. Throwing everything into the boot of her car, she closed the lid knowing she was doing the right thing.

The bonfire was huge and burned with intense heat. The statues she'd so conscientiously worshipped exploded in the flames. When the fire subsided, all that remained was ash and fragments of pottery; so closing a large chapter of Marina's life.

Far from fading, as Angelo had hoped, Marina's spiritual life with Jesus grew stronger. Reading her Bible at least daily and speaking to Jesus throughout the day, may seem strange to some, but that's what she did. Her relationship with Jesus was deepening. She found His love hard to explain. As the weeks passed by, Marina, rightly or wrongly, sensed one aspect of her relationship with Angelo was not in keeping with her new life. She loved him and he her. They were in love, partners, and best friends. He was part of her life - a comfort in times of trouble. They were a cohesive unit.

Finding a way to tell Angelo she'd found a greater love in Jesus and wanted to curtail her physical relationship with him and yet remain his friend was difficult. They'd shared their dreams, aspirations and desires with each other, but this was different. *What can I do? In whom can I confide or trust to help me with such a personal dilemma?* Her answer was sure and steadfast. He who gave His life for her, He who'd lifted her out of her idolatrous bondage, He who answered her prayers and held her in the palm of His hand: Jesus was the only one to whom she could turn. For weeks, she agonised in prayer; asking for strength and courage to tell Angelo that she only wanted to be his friend. She knew to raise the subject at the wrong time or in the wrong way could destroy their relationship and in so doing alienate him from the very one she yearned for him to meet - Jesus. She'd experienced the height of love that Jesus generates; a love far beyond human measure, the unearned love that God has for humanity [agape love]. She'd felt the glory of His divine Presence [Shekinah] that human words fail to express adequately. She wondered if she could find the right words to say without ambiguity. She considered she had a good English vocabulary as did Angelo, but her mother tongue was Portuguese and his was Italian. Placing her faith in Jesus to be with her, and to give her the right words to say, courageously she told him how she felt about her Saviour and that her love for him remained unchanged.

Angelo knew nothing of such spiritual love nor could she expect him to understand. But human love has the capacity and the power to rise far above expectation, for when Marina told him how she loved Jesus and that now she wanted only to be his friend, adding she truly loved him, his love for her hit the heights of understanding. He loved her deeply, but now his love for her soared far beyond human reasoning. A gigantic decision faced Angelo - lose her or bide his time until the enthusiasm for her new interest wore off. Rather than lose her, he agreed to remain her best friend and live apart. Lingering in the depths of his mind was the belief that she'd soon dump religion when issues that were more pressing caught her imagination. Taking a room in the hotel, he hoped their friendship would survive and her religious craze would quickly pass. Not fully accepting her thinking, Angelo displayed a love that few can endure. Setting deep physical contact aside, he continued to support, advise and encourage her in all that she sought to do. How long her fanciful religion would last was anyone's guess.

9
Renegade

Marina's relationship with Angelo was now firmly on a platonic footing. Angelo's attendance at church continued in body only. Up the steps, through the door and onto the back pew he sneaked to sleep; oblivious of the people and their worship. He thought by suffering a couple of hours a week on a hard pew to keep Marina happy for the rest of the week was worth it. He was content to 'nod off' until she'd had her fix of religion. He'd had enough of this love stuff to last him a lifetime. He wanted no part of it. He was there for Marina, and no one else.

One particular Sunday, as the service got underway, he closed his eyes; desperate to shut out the worship and the Word. He dosed for a while. He could see and hear quite clearly his aunts and uncles saying, 'Everything will be fine. You'll have a good time. There'll be lots of boys of your age.'

Angelo's stomach churned at the memory - more likely the beer he'd drunk the previous night. His dozing deepened as the worship continued. Present in body, he was far away, reliving memories of the distant past.

'You'll love boarding school,' assured his mum.

Angelo did not share her enthusiasm. The isolation and loneliness he'd felt when at summer school had been enough for him. Pictures of the one-storey L-shaped building overlooking a large square play area surrounded by high wire fencing facing a roadway brought depressing memories. He did not relish the idea of spending three long years in such a foreboding place. This would be no vacation. Slipping deeper into a world of hurtful memories, he could see nuns standing in the grounds directing the children inside. 'I have to go, now, Angelo,' he heard his mum say.

Suppressing his longing to return home, the eight year old bravely held back his tears as he watched with heavy heart the mini bus take his mother away. As soon as the vehicle had gone, his older brother whom he'd been assured would be with him, was escorted to another part of the building.

His acute sense of loneliness took hold when seeing the huge dormitory of fifteen to twenty beds that was to be his home. That night he slipped beneath the covers and let his tears flow trying hard to smother the sound of his crying. After many hours, he finally slept. His private lament continued for many nights.

Angelo bent to the daily routine of prayers at seven, breakfast [caffè latte or hot chocolate] and then lessons until dinnertime. More lessons filled the afternoon. After tea, more prayers followed. Eight-thirty was bedtime along with the imposed strict regime of silence until dawn. He'd been happy and free as a bird at home and was now lonely and confined. His only source of comfort, a constant refrain of reassurance rang loudly in his head. *My mum and dad will visit at the weekend.*

Determined to make the best of the enforced separation, he quickly made friends. The first Saturday, a buzz of excitement filled the air as homesick children rushed to the fencing to await their parents' arrival. Gripping the wire, he and his brother watched as parent after parent rushed to kiss their children and dish out the food they'd brought. Time slowly ticked away as Angelo longed to see his mum and dad.

'They'll be held up in all the traffic,' said his brother seeing a number of adults leaving.

He got the message. 'They're not coming, are they?'

'I don't think so. Perhaps they'll come next week.'

Keeping hope alive, he clung to the fence. A deep void opened within him when seeing the last of the parents leave and the caretaker lock the gates.

'Come along!' shouted a nun waving to those children standing at the wire barrier. Angelo released his grip and headed for the building; occasionally glancing back, yearning, longing and hoping to see his mum standing there. The monotonous routine of early rising, prayers, washing, eating, lessons, eating, lessons, prayer and bedtime continued.

The following Saturday was nothing more than a repeat of the previous, with Angelo and his brother clinging to the fencing. When their parents failed to arrive, all sorts of weird and irrational thoughts gripped his impressionable mind. The idea that he'd been abandoned marred his thinking. He felt unloved and longed to feel his mother's arms around him. Experiencing the cruel mind taunts of parental rejection and sensing acute loneliness, all manner of depressive thoughts took root. Young as he was, exhausting the destructive power of self-pity, the powerful defence mechanism of rationalisation captured his reasoning. *How can they travel all this way? Dad is up by four each morning and never in bed before one. How can I expect him to visit? He's busy building a business for my brothers and me.* The same work ethic was true of his mum - baking, cooking,

cleaning and tending to the business. *How selfish I am.*
They'll visit when they can.

By the third weekend, Angelo's hope of seeing his
parents bubbled within him. *Perhaps they'll visit today.*
They did not come. Three arduous weeks stretched in
to three long years as each Saturday, the few unbearable
hours of gazing towards the road came to nothing. His
dad never visited. His mum rarely came. It never
occurred to him that his parents believed they were
doing their best by providing a good education. With
this deep wound etched on his mind, the scar would
take many years if not a lifetime to heal.

Determined to shut out all things spiritual when
dozing in the pew, Angelo had unwittingly directed his
thoughts to hurtful memories. Seeking comfort in his
dreamy state, he was back at boarding school indulging
in more of his past. Lost in his imagination, he was in
the school's large dining room, with its high roof, wide
planked floorboards and half-panelled wooden walls.
The furnishing was more akin to an eighteenth century
workhouse with its long wooden tables, hard benches
and austere environment. He half smiled in his
dreaming when catching sight of the nuns standing like
prison guards silently watching each child approach the
table that housed a number of trays and canisters of hot
food. His eyes met those of the well-fed server as she
flung a dollop of lumpy semolina into his bowl - much
like a worker flinging wet cement from a trowel. He
detested the stuff and protested.

A tall slender nun nearby caught his expression and
heard his disgruntled sigh. 'Eat it and be grateful,' she
snapped, shooing him away. Angelo's hesitation held up

the line of hungry children. 'Get back to your table and be thankful you have food to fill your belly.'

Back in his seat, he sat staring at the soggy dessert. Others with a similar dislike for the pudding raised their objections. He glanced across the table at his friend. A cheeky grin filled his face. Plunging his spoon into the semolina, he flicked the mush at him.

'Hey! What do you think you're playing at?' the boy screamed, wiping the mess from his eye.

The return fire was swift. Others joined in the mêlée. Soon the dining room was alive with energetic laughter as the thick milky substance splattered the walls, floor, benches and clothing.

'Stop it! Stop!' screamed a flustered nun, out of her depth in dealing with rebellion.

The fracas continued as unruly children laughed, shouted and screamed at one another; releasing their pent up frustrations. Some were fighting.

'Stop it!' bellowed a large stocky priest rushing into the hall followed by an entourage of female re-enforcement, each displaying an urgency to quash the riotous delinquents. No genteel love prevailed that day. The action was swift. Heavy hands parted the culprits and forceful slaps subdued the defiant children. Peace restored, the priest cast his eyes over the offenders then bellowed in a deep vibrating voice. 'Which one of you felons started the rumpus?'

No one dared move or speak until a little sneak pointed timidly at Angelo, mumbling under his breath, 'He did.'

'You spoke, boy! Did you start the fray?'

The boy gulped. Pointing to Angelo, he trembled. 'No, Papa. It - it was him.'

In rage, the priest with his fiery eyes ablaze, lifted Angelo bodily off the bench by his ears and on to his feet.

Enduring the excruciating pain, Angelo was determined not to let the big fellow see his suffering.

'Get this mess cleaned up!' demanded the priest. 'The rest of you can go. Go on. Get out! There'll be no more food for you lot today!'

A scurry of feet headed for the door. A nun who was standing cross-armed flung a cloth at Angelo, huffed and then departed.

When everyone had gone, the priest gave his full attention to Angelo, forcing him to his knees. 'I'll teach you not to throw food around.' Under the watchful eye of the priestly figure, it took him hours to clean the mess. He'd almost finished when the big fellow yelled, 'That will do!'

Thinking he was done and wanting to rest, he was surprised when the priest grabbed his collar and frog marched him out into the centre of the play area.

'Now we'll see what you're made of. Squat, boy! Squat!' Too frightened to protest, he cowered under the priest's dominance. 'Place your hands palm downwards on the ground! Hurry now! I don't have all day. Inward, boy! Inward! Turn your hands inward!' Not daring to look up and holding back his tears, Angelo obeyed. 'Now stay there until I tell you to move.'

The squatting position, with hands turned inward and palms touching the ground, is not a comfortable position to be in for hours on end. But hours rather than minutes was his punishment by way of penitence. Cramp in his fingers, wrists, elbows, knees and ankles, he quickly felt the pain. Only when the hot day faded and the chilled night air slipped into the valley did the punishment end. Painful joints along with muscle cramps served only to indelibly imprint the ordeal on his mind.

Some nuns thought the misplaced chastisement imposed by authority was far too excessive when weighed against a childish prank performed by a vulnerable eight-year-old. Far more damage than physical pain erupted that day. The severe punishment served only to drive a deeper wedge between him and the church. Love, compassion, caring and forgiveness were not attributes which were readily in abundance at that place. If they were, Angelo rarely saw them.

The strict organisational rules as experienced by Angelo, continued unabated. Yet despite his suffering, an ulterior motive found him in active service at the local place of worship. Each Sunday, the entire school populace marched along the road to the local church which was a somewhat elaborate building within walking distance of the school. What enticed Angelo into dutiful participation was not born of any religious zeal or the wearing of a cassock. Neither Jesus nor the many saints of that faith was the motivator - food was the reason. He'd seen how those who helped the priest during the service were afterwards treated to a feast. A chance to fill his stomach on things not seen at school took his fancy. To avoid missing out, he volunteered his services. Angelo made sure he ate his fill. He enjoyed swinging the incense and helping the big fellow at the mass. This was the first time he felt an urge to serve others. Not only did he feel privileged, he also felt important. How long this saintly masquerade would last was anyone's guess.

Believing him to be contrite, the priest was pleased to see the boy bending to his will.

Meanwhile, Angelo was far away from the reality of the on-going church service that Marina was enjoying in praise, prayer and listening to what the pastor had to say. Busily reliving rebellion, he was distant from heavenly thoughts or spiritual desires.

Well into his school term, and lacking money to buy stationery, he approached his friends, 'I'm short of writing paper. Can I have some of yours?'

'No chance. I'm on my last few pages,' said one.

'Buy some from the school shop,' said another.

'What with? I've no money.'

'Me neither,' said the first.

'We could lift some,' said a fourth.

'How do you mean?' asked Angelo.

'You know. We'll take what we want.'

'Don't be stupid. That's stealing.'

'Think of it as a loan. We'll pay for it when we've the cash. There's a loose pane of glass in the shop door. It won't take us long to lever it out. It's only held by a nail.'

'What if we're caught?' asked the first.

'We'll confess. What can they do to us? If we appear contrite, we won't have much repenting to do. Who cares about us?'

Angelo was desperate. 'Sounds good to me.'

After the shop had closed, and in a brief respite from regimental routine, two kept watch while Angelo and one other sneaked down the corridor to the shop door. He gently prised the loose glass from the window frame. Slipping his hand through the gap, he turned the lock and pushed the door open before gesturing to the others to follow him. Closing the door, they feasted their eyes on an array of writing material and books.

'Shush! There's someone coming,' whispered Angelo. Hoping no one would notice the missing pane, the four scurried behind the counter. Angelo squatted on the floor as the sound of feet passed the shop doorway. The seconds of silence seemed like an eternity. 'They've gone.'

With eager hands and greedy eyes, each helped themselves to what they wanted. One of the boys felt nervy. 'We'd best go before someone finds us.'

'Hey, there's cash in here,' said Angelo opening a drawer. 'Shall I take it?'

'Yeah! Why not?'

Thankful that no one had seen them, Angelo pocketed the coins and then slipped away with the others. Later that evening, pleased with their hoard, the boys stood in church singing hymns with their faces pictures of innocence.

After the last hymn, everyone sat waiting for the priest to give his fatherly advice mingled with vague threats. The priest walked to the front of the church and faced the congregation. His face set, as if to declare some catastrophic disaster, he sombrely announced, 'Someone has broken into the school shop and taken goods and money.'

A gasp of disbelief arose from the pews as everyone looked accusingly at his or her neighbour.

The priest set his eyes on those seated on the front row and then scanned the rest of the congregation. 'How evil! How evil that someone or some persons could do such an act! Never in all the years as a priest have I known such abomination. It's outrageous. Truly outrageous. We have a thief or thieves amongst us. May they not rest until having publically confessed their ill deeds. I demand that whoever is responsible stand before me right now and repent of their crime. If not, I'll send for the police. They'll not be as kind as I am.' The four sat silently not daring to look at each other. 'Have it your own way, thief or thieves. The police it shall be.'

Angelo's guilt held him to ransom. His whole body shook. He felt physically sick at the thought of what might happen to him if the police got involved. He doubted if he could trust the others to keep their mouths shut. By the end of the service, he felt heavily burdened. While everyone was leaving, still shaking, he walked to the front of the church and stood before the priest. 'I took the stationery and money from the shop,' admitted Angelo with his head bowed low in contrition.

The priest towered dominantly over him. Raising Angelo's chin with his finger, he fixed his piercing dark brown eyes upon the boy. 'Did you now?' he said in a frightening tone. 'You'd best give me the cash and everything else you stole.'

'I will, Papa. I will.' He stood waiting for the punishment.

'Go, and don't do anything like that ever again,' came the deathly warning.

'I won't, Papa.' Angelo was amazed that one minute the priest could be so cruel and the next so kind. Despite the unexpected outcome, he was thankful he'd avoided public humiliation and a police record.

Drawn back from his dreaming at the sound of the congregation singing, Angelo jumped to his feet hoping that no one had seen him dozing. Marina gave him a wry smile. After the service, he slipped quietly away.

10

The Promise

Angelo knew he was in for a long haul when Marina announced, 'I'm going to be baptised in water by total immersion.'

He gulped. Where does this baptism come from? It's a bit strange to me. Why does she want to be dipped in water? What next will it be? She has this Jesus thing in a big way. 'Why do you want to get dunked in water? Weren't you christened when you were a baby?'

'I was. Water baptism is the act of dying to your old self and leaving the past behind. It's a cleansing and a rising to a new birth,' said Marina. Jesus was baptised in the River Jordan by his cousin.'

'You're not going to Israel, are you?'

'I'd love too, but it's a bit too far at the moment. I have a choice - be baptised in the church baptistery - or in the sea.'

'You must be mad. The sea will be freezing.'

'Stop exaggerating. Jesus said, "Whoever believes and is baptised will be saved."' She wanted to add, *but whoever does not believe will be condemned,* but thought she'd said enough.

'How much is this baptism going to cost you?'

'Nothing!'

'Nothing! I thought it would cost you a few pounds at the least. You don't get anything free in this life.'

'You're wrong, Angelo. Salvation is free. If people could buy salvation and a place in Heaven with cash, it would be overbooked for those with enough money to pay. No! That is not God's way. We're redeemed at a price and that price was Jesus, God's only son. Jesus paid for our redemption when shedding His blood on a cross for every one of us, without exception. Death could not hold Him. God raised Jesus from the grave, and took Him into Heaven and He is now actively involved in the lives of those who love Him.

'Show me.'

'I can't. You have to ask Jesus into your life.' Since meeting with Jesus, she'd realised those who have a personal relationship with Him often fail when taking their eyes off Him. 'You don't need me to tell you that no one can force anyone to love them. Love can only be given by the giver and accepted only at the receiver's will. When Jesus became my close Friend, you know how my life changed. Jesus could not live in me if my sinful nature had continued as it had done before meeting Him. I've told you long enough that Jesus abhors sin but not the sinner. He died for sinners - for you and for me.'

Angelo recoiled behind his protective barricade.

Marina's baptismal day finally arrived. A Sunday, there was a buzz of excitement in the air and the sun shone in a cloudless sky as the congregation walked the short distance from the church to the beach. The sea was far out when the worshippers arrived to witness the event. The four women about to be baptised were thankful that the church had hired a chalet where they could get dry and dressed after the event.

There was lots of laughter and excitement as the crowd gathered in a half circle on the sand to sing gospel songs and pray before heading seaward to watch the baptisms. With much enthusiasm and a touch of apprehension as to the temperature of the sea, the candidates, each in flimsy apparel, set off to experience a once in a lifetime occasion.

The preacher was already standing waist high in his wetsuit beaming with delight despite the cold water. The sea glistened like a huge lake as the first to be baptised waded into the water.

To ensure everyone's safety, a helper stood opposite the minister ready to lift the baptised from the water. There was great rejoicing when the first emerged from the sea. Then it was Marina's turn to be baptised. Standing between the preacher and his assistant, she placed her hands across her chest as words of instruction and reassurance fell from the preacher's lips.

'I baptise you in the name of the Father, Son and Holy Spirit.'

Under the waves she went; totally immersed. Firm arms dragged her from the waves. Thoroughly drenched and wiping the water from her eyes, she beamed ecstatically. Praising Jesus, out of the sea she ran.

The whole event had been a memorable occasion for those being baptised, and a reminder to others of the time when they too had passed through the waters of baptism.

The congregation then prayed for the passers-by who'd watched the event from a distance. They prayed that the unsure, the hesitant, the doubters, the rejecters of a Creator God would one day recall what they'd seen and ask Jesus into their lives.

At church the following Sunday, Marina spoke of how Jesus had brought meaning to her life. She was so excited at having been baptised, she looked forward to other joys of a spiritual nature. Angelo knew this was no passing fancy.

Not long after her baptism, Marina was praying with Gill when she received the promise of the Holy Spirit. She began to praise God in a spiritual tongue.

When Angelo heard her speaking a new tongue which he did not understand, he thought she'd gone crazy. He worried as to where all this religious stuff would lead her. He'd heard and seen enough. It unnerved him. Inwardly feeling fearful, he withdrew. He was content and determined not to let anything disturb the way he lived his life.

As the weeks passed, Marina was keen to share the love of Jesus with her family in Brazil, especially her mum. After the summer season in England, she packed her bags and headed for South America. Her relatives were thrilled to see her but had difficulty understanding her new religion which is what they understood it to be. Marina had a hard time explaining the relationship she now had with Jesus. They knew well her old ways, and while not fully understanding what had happened to her, they could see she'd changed for the better. Having been in South America for a few weeks, as she entered a shop Marina came face to face with the one she had found in bed with her ex-boyfriend.

A natural reaction may well have been to experience an adrenaline rush or a churning and burning in her stomach. She felt none of these. Hot sweats, trembling, bristling of the hairs on the back of her neck, the setting of the teeth were all absent. She felt at peace. A desire to hurt may well have been her reaction had she not known Jesus. Confrontation and revenge were far from her thoughts. She'd read, *Do not take revenge, my friends, but leave room for God's wrath, for it is written: 'It is mine to avenge; I will repay,' says the Lord. On the contrary: 'If your enemy is hungry, feed him; if he is thirsty, give him something to drink. In doing this, you will heap burning coals on his head'* (Romans 12:19-20).

There in the shop, Marina faced her past knowing Jesus was with her. She was not about to forfeit God's Presence in Christ Jesus to avenge past hurts. She recalled words in her Bible: *No, in all these things we are more than conquerors through him who loved us. For I am convinced that neither death nor life, neither angels nor demons, neither the present nor the future, nor any powers, neither height nor depth, nor anything else in all creation, will be able to separate us from the love of God that is in Christ Jesus our Lord* Romans 8:37-39).

Peace and compassion for the woman overwhelmed Marina. Forgiveness for past hurts abounded. Where a deep-seated loathing had dwelt, sadness and sorrow for the lost soul brought her to tears. Love had conquered. On leaving the shop, overwhelming copious tears drenched her face.

While at her mum's house, a festive atmosphere filled the town. High on a hilltop, a celebration was in full swing as the townsfolk gathered around a huge effigy of a saint. Marina sensed deep sorrow for the people as they bowed and prayed to the statue. She wanted to cry out, 'It's made by human hands. It's a stone. Jesus is The Way The Truth and The Life. God doesn't want you to worship or adore anyone or anything. Jesus is the only way to God.' In her despair for the people, she recalled the first commandment: '*You shall have no other gods before me. You shall not make for yourself an idol in the form of anything in heaven above or on the earth beneath or in the waters below. You shall not bow down to them or worship them…*' (Exodus 20:3-5).

Her heart wept for the people. In her anguish, she praised God that she'd met Jesus. Sad for the people, she'd read in her Bible, *Therefore, since Christ suffered in his body, arm yourselves also with the same attitude, because he who has suffered in his body is done with sin. As a result, he does not live the rest of his earthly life for evil human desires, but rather for the will of God. For you have spent enough time in the past doing what pagans choose to do - living in debauchery, lust, drunkenness, orgies, carousing and detestable idolatry* (1 Peter 4:1-3*).*

Her thoughts drifted momentarily to the time she too had been far from God - lost in venerating idols. Still sad for the people, she recalled the following verses:

They think it strange that you do not plunge with them into the same flood of dissipation, and they heap abuse on you. But they will have to give account to him who is ready to judge the living and the dead. For this is the reason the gospel was preached even to those who are now dead, so that they might be judged according to men in regard to the body, but live according to God in regard to the spirit (1 Peter 4:4-6).

In the midst of her heartache, she thanked Jesus for directing her to burn the statues and paraphernalia that had kept her bound for so long.

On her way back to her mum's house, she lovingly explained to her friends how she felt and shared the gospel message. Sadly, they continued to hold firm to their traditions. Marina took comfort in knowing that God's Word will not return unto Him empty (Isaiah 55:11). She prayed earnestly that one day the Truth would set them free (John 8:32). Trusting Jesus that He would direct her in the way he would have her go, she returned to England.

Angelo continued to shut out the things of God. He did not understand what Marina experienced; nor did he make any effort to find out. According to him, whatever strange thing she had, was her thing - not his. He was pleased she was happy and was looked forward to the time when the novelty wore off. He had no desire to seek or run after another woman. However, as a vulnerable male, on hearing the plight of another female, he was swept off his feet and his heart set alight with a new love.

11

The Other Woman

Angelo had not yet reached the point where he considered his self-imposed lifestyle to be a problem. Like many who indulge themselves, he was oblivious to the subliminal effects his routine was having on his health. Despite Marina telling him the gospel message whenever she returned from study and prayer with Gill, he would have none of it. He was like a medieval knight who was secure in his castle and surrounded not by one protective wall but by many: a place where nothing could hurt him. His security misplaced, little did he know his keep was vulnerable. Already his enemies were active within him. The protection he'd surrounded himself with was not kind, gentle or loving. He'd built his stronghold with a wall of drugs, a wall of drink and a wall of gambling that would, if not demolished, result in his ultimate destruction; a death of his own making. He'd no time for Jesus. There was no place for a Saviour in his castle. Despite him attending church with Marina, the narrow road that starts with Jesus lay firmly on the outside of his fortress. He refused to hear the gospel message. Determined to resist God's love from whatever source, be it song, word or action, he held his shield high to shut out Jesus' voice.

In church, he'd not quite settled down to sleep when the preacher's words hit him hard. 'Open your closed heart and let Jesus into your life.' He knew the words were for him. Caught off guard, he resisted with a rationalisation. *I'm not a bad lad.* Lifting his protective shield higher, he closed his ears and eyes and was off to sleep.

The weeks rolled into months. Angelo's resistance to all things spiritual, hardened. He felt safe away from church; more himself - relaxed and free. He decided that no one was going to catch him off guard ever again. He raised his protective barriers well before entering any church. He'd even considered not going with Marina to the Sunday services, but had not quite made up his mind.

One summer's evening, his thoughts were far from spiritual matters when an old acquaintance visited his restaurant. Angelo was busy cooking when he happened to glance through the window. His heart trembled on seeing the man approach the restaurant carrying a small case.

'Oh no! Not him!' His instinct was to run, but he had meals to cook. 'Not now! No. Not now!' He acted as if Al Capone had ordered his assassination and the contract was about to be fulfilled.

A concerned employee noticed his erratic behaviour. 'Are you okay, Angelo?'

'I'm fine,' he replied, not daring to take his eyes off the hit man. 'He's coming in,' he muttered. Sure enough, the stocky built, clean-shaven Italian, with longish dark hair and brown shifty eyes, entered as if stepping out of a gangster movie.

'Table for one,' he said, in a strong commanding voice and then sat near the front window at a table for six. Placing his case on the floor, he looked around suspiciously. He spied Angelo peeping through the serving hatch. Not a muscle did the man move when acknowledged with a hesitant wave. Angelo tried to concentrate on cooking but his hands were shaking and his stomach churned like a cement mixer. *What's he doing here? What's he after? He'll be up to no good.*

His visitor feared no one and possessed an unpredictable fiery temper which was ignited by the most minuscule distraction. Known as an unsavoury character who was both dreaded and respected, Angelo recalled how the man often carried stacks of money in his suitcase. From where he acquired the cash, none dared ask. He tried to concentrate on cooking the meals while keeping a watchful eye on his visitor. Not fully focusing on the task in hand, he recalled the time they'd worked together in one of the town's restaurants. One particular memory stood out from similar incidents. The visitor, Angelo and one other had been preparing food. The man could not concentrate due to the third making too much noise. Suddenly he picked up a carving knife, grabbed the culprit's neck and held him over a hot stove. 'I'll slit your throat if you don't shut your face!' Drawn back to reality, Angelo had no urge to speak with his visitor but knew he'd have to at least say, 'Hello.' He checked to see if he was still there. His heart sank on seeing him order a meal. A lull in the kitchen prompted Angelo to pluck up courage to go speak to him. 'Hi, Luciano. How are things?' Luciano's fiery eyes penetrated Angelo's safe zone. He felt threatened. *I don't like this at all. How do I get rid of him?* He trembled when Luciano reached for his case and lifted the lid sufficiently to finger the contents. Angelo followed his every move; not knowing what to expect - a knife, a gun, drugs or cash. *Surely, he'll not try anything in here - not while the restaurant is full.* He searched his mind for anything he'd done to arouse the visitor's anger.

'Got it,' said Luciano slamming a book on the table. 'It's this you want,' he said passionately.

Angelo glanced at the book half covered by the man's hand. *The guy's crazy.*

A wide friendly smile filled Luciano's face. 'It's Jesus you need. It's Jesus you need.'

Angelo relaxed at the sight of a Bible. He thought Luciano had banged his head or perhaps had a serious accident or a breakdown of some sort, then silently remarked, *Another crank like Marina.*

Luciano was not crazed. He'd not banged his head, been in an accident or suffered any psychological breakdown. Of sound mind, he'd met with Jesus. He spoke with authority to get the message of Jesus' love across to a resistant colleague. 'God still loves you, Angelo. Why don't you love him?' He had no answer. Luciano had not lost his forceful voice although his fiery temper was gone. 'It's Jesus you need, Angelo. It's Jesus you need!'

Angelo listened intently as Luciano continued to speak about Jesus' love.

'I go to church,' he hesitantly confessed.

'That's great! You're almost there,' said Luciano thumping his Bible to emphasise the urgency of his words. 'Go to church, you say! That's good. It's a start. It's Jesus you need!'

Angelo omitted to say that when in church he closed his ears to the things of God and slept throughout the service. The two talked a little longer. Well, Luciano certainly did. Angelo said, somewhat half-heartedly, hoping he'd not take up the invitation, 'You must come again sometime. I'll cook you a meal.'

'I will,' smiled the feisty Italian. 'Can I bring my family?'

'Sure!' He would have agreed to anything to get rid of him. As more people arrived, he excused himself and returned to the kitchen. Luciano slipped his Bible into his case, enjoyed his meal and left.

While obvious to Angelo that Luciano had undergone a massive change of heart, he personally did not intend to open his ears or heart to Jesus' voice. A few Sundays later, one of those hot summer's days most likely to entice a believer to skip worship and walk on the sandy beach, Angelo arrived at church in his usual frame of mind; hoping no-one would bother him. He wanted to sleep. Slipping into a back pew, his eyes caught sight of an unfamiliar face. *That's strange. Where's the regular chap? Who's this fellow dressed in peculiar gear?* He was curious. *Maybe I can listen to him instead of sleeping.* The preacher, a man of Pakistani origin dressed in his national costume was entertaining and made Angelo laugh.

He listened to him tell of how a large crowd had gathered around Jesus; pushing and shoving their way to get close to Him. A woman had been in the crowd. She'd been haemorrhaging for twelve years and had spent all her money on doctor's fees in search of a cure. Seeing Jesus, she knew if she touched Him, she'd be healed. She pushed her way through the bustling crowd towards Him. When near enough, she touched His garment and knew instantly she was well. Jesus felt power drain from Him and asked, *Who touched my clothes?'* Trembling with fear, the woman, confessed. Jesus said, *'Daughter, your faith has healed you. Go in peace and be free from your suffering'* (Mark 5:34). The preacher didn't talk long and then invited those requesting prayer to step forward.

Fixed firmly to his seat, Angelo had not missed a word the visitor had said. Suddenly, he felt a strong force stirring deep within him. His heart pounded as the mysterious power intensified. Knowing he could not remain seated and that to touch Jesus would make a difference, such was the overwhelming power that he now experienced he cried out in mind, *I must go and ask for prayer!* Such was the intensity, Angelo could not contain his longing and within seconds was standing before the man.

Marina was surprised to see him at the front. 'Thank you, Jesus. Thank you.' She'd prayed hard for this moment.

'Do you wish me to pray for you?' the man asked.

Deeply immersed in the indescribable force that had lifted him from his pew, he was speechless. The visitor placed his hand over Angelo's heart and then prayed.

Closing his eyes, a warm glow filled his body. Immersed in an overwhelming sense of peace, he suddenly dropped to the floor. His eyes shut, Angelo witnessed black smoke pour out of him and white enter. Immediately he felt good, transformed and at ease. He lay outstretched for some time basking in God's love. Opening his eyes, he was shocked to find himself stretched out on the floor. Experiencing the touch of the Holy Spirit, he felt different. 'Wow! I feel so light.' He smiled when getting up. *This feeling is so nice. Something*

117

has happened inside me. I sense *good things like being clean inside.* He was excited. *It's real. Jesus is real. Before it seemed as though everyone was acting to make money. Now I know it's true. Jesus loves me.*

There had been no coercion or forced direction to please, reward or satisfy some other's ego. Angelo had closed his eyes and especially his ears to the things of God when sleeping in the pews. His desire to ask Jesus into his life had come not by any man's or woman's persuasive tongue as the drugs had come, but by God's Spirit working silently within his life showing him that there is a better way of living; a new exciting way - a way that can and does change lives. Through acceptance by faith that Jesus carried his sins by dying for him on a cross at a place called Calvary, Angelo knew he was no longer alone. He now had Jesus with him. Sadly however, his addictions were not to depart so easily.

12

Blessings and Conflicts

Accepting that Jesus died a cruel death for his wilfulness was a major step forward for Angelo. With little knowledge of what it meant to know Jesus, he'd much to learn about his Saviour. Even after asking Jesus into his life, he was rebellious and defiant to a point where his ravenous cravings were keen to rob him of his blessings. Shortly after he'd met Jesus, the temptation to gamble got the better of him. Off he went to the betting shop. Placing his bet, Marina happened to pass by and saw him. Without thought of the consequences, she dragged him out by his ear.

'Ouch! That hurt!' squealed Angelo. 'Why do that?'

'You shouldn't be in there! What would Jesus say?'

She had tried many times to lovingly convey to Angelo that since he'd invited Jesus to be with him, he had to think seriously as to the way he lived his life. Her action at the betting shop was born out of frustration and concern. Violence was not her way. Her desire was to show love, tolerance and patience. She was at her wits end as to what she should do. Weeks later, despite her concern for Angelo's spiritual welfare, his temptation to gamble intensified. Marina was at the hotel when he said, 'I'm going out for a few minutes.'

His brazen expression aroused her suspicions. 'If you're going to that betting shop, I'll smack you,' she said with a smile.

Finding her remarks amusing, he sniggered and sloped off without saying a word. He was standing in a packed betting shop watching the horseracing on the big screen when Marina appeared at the door.

'I told you not to come here. It's wrong!' she yelled. Rushing in, she slipped headlong onto the floor. Angelo was out of the back door; not realising she'd fallen. A number of punters rushed to help her, sniggering at her predicament. Unhurt and embarrassed, she stormed out.

To them, she was a nagging woman intent on stopping her man from enjoying himself. No one knew she loved Jesus and was trying to stop Angelo from slipping back into his old ways. She'd done her best both physically and verbally to stop him from gambling. She'd prayed hard for him to meet Jesus. Now that he had, she prayed that Jesus would remove his addictions. Her answer came swiftly and in such a profound way - direct intervention. While Marina, Gill and Zoraida, her Venezuelan friend, prayed for Angelo, he again slipped out to gamble. It was the day the transparent, impenetrable, steel shutter had dropped between him and the entrance.

Fixed to the spot, Angelo reeled in anger. *What's wrong with me? I need to place my bet.* Again, he tried to enter but could not move. A voice from deep within him cried, *Stop! No more. That's it. You cannot go there ever again.* His stubborn defiance took hold along with an obstinate silent cry. *I came to have a bet, and that's what I'll do!* He knew what he wanted and was determined to do things his way. There in the street, a battle of wills raged - a battle he must win. Much like the excitement of placing a bet, this time there was more at stake than winning or losing a few pounds. Again, he tried to step forward but could not move. He was resolved more than ever to enter. Yet again, as he took a step forward, his feet were anchored to the pavement. Defiant, determined and rebellious, he battled with the voice until a chink in his armour of obstinacy appeared. *Do I gamble or go home?* It was decision time. *I'll place my bet tomorrow.* Conceding, calmness washed over him as his frustration, anxiety and anger crumbled. At peace, he turned for home; confident that he would never again enter such an establishment or place a bet.

Angelo's spiritual battle had been as real as any conflict fought with conventional weaponry. He hadn't been shot, knifed, beaten up or taken prisoner. He remained free to go his own way. He'd lost the fight that his stubbornness had waged. He knew well, with God's help, he'd won a significant victory. The chains that had bound him for so long to an addictive practice were broken. The betting shop was not for him. Thankful for heeding the inner voice, he was happy yet unaware that his other addictions would not willingly release their grip on his life.

Had he not experienced Jesus' Presence at that time, Angelo would have accepted the event as fate. As to the timing of the women's prayer, that it was chance or just a fluke may well have been his thinking. Aware that 'coincidence' is an easy answer that satisfies the mind, eases the conscience and lays a matter to rest, he considered not only the mechanics of the incident, but the realism of the moment, along with what he'd heard, sensed and felt. Concluding that God had indeed stopped him from entering the betting shop, then and only then did the negative persistent stubbornness that had plagued him throughout his life, change to a positive driving force for good.

Prior to knowing Jesus, Angelo knew only what others had told him as a child and what little he'd learned about Jesus as an adult. He'd experienced religion, a creed, a belief - not a personal living relationship with a loving Saviour. He'd experienced and rejected the mechanistic ritualistic format of worship. His perception of such was fixed from early days as a way of seducing the vulnerable, controlling the unruly, comforting the weary and sucking up to the rich and those in authority. He had not yet discovered that knowing Jesus is not a religion but a way to the heart of God's love - an exciting vibrant life and a consuming adventure which reaches out to those who do not know the love and pleasure of being in Jesus' presence.

The desire to gamble had ended in a very dramatic way. As for his beer drinking, the temptation intensified. Submitting to his intense longing to taste a beer, he opened a can and drank. Immediately, he felt excruciating pain in his stomach. The next time he tried, the same happened; accompanied by a heavy weight pressing down hard on his belly. Not fully understanding the power of prayer, Angelo asked the Pakistani preacher named Ali who was visiting the church to pray that his intense craving for beer would leave him. After Ali prayed for him, he decided not to touch beer ever again.

Like New Year's resolutions, good intentions melt into insignificance when temptation raises its head. A week later, free from pain, Angelo surrendered to his urge and sneaked a beer. Taking one small sip, the pain he'd previously experienced returned with vengeance. Suddenly, he felt the Presence of the Spirit of God working in him. *That's enough. Stop drinking.* He'd heard the same voice outside the betting shop. He had no doubt as to who had spoken to him. Instantly, his intense desire to drink beer left him. His cannabis smokes lingered. He had not yet read: *They promise them freedom, while they themselves are slaves of depravity - for a man is a slave to whatever has mastered him* (2 Peter 2:19).

Marina, John, Gill and many others continued to pray for Angelo's release from his addiction. His break with cannabis came much more easily to him than that for drinking and gambling. The temptation to drink and gamble was all around him. For Angelo, smoking cannabis was a private activity and while easily obtained, once his supply ran out, he abandoned the weed. Now free from all controlling cravings, he earnestly sought Jesus by opening his heart and life fully to his loving Saviour. Prayer and reading his Italian Bible came naturally to him. He was overjoyed that his body was cleansed of self-inflicted poisons and now filled with a love he'd never known before: a spiritual love freely given by a loving Heavenly Father - Creator God.

Angelo had closed his eyes and ears to Jesus for years. Now he'd met with Him, he knew that His Saviour was no figment of imagination. He had first-hand experience of a living relationship with Jesus. He'd discovered that the 'great delusion', as people would have had him believe, is not God, but man's fascination with primate development. He loved Jesus and there was no reason why he should not be baptised. John and Gill encouraged him to study the Bible with them. He was keen to attend and soaked up the teaching. John invited him to an Alpha Course to which he agreed.

An Alpha Course gives people an opportunity to explore the Christian faith over ten weekly sessions in a relaxed setting.

Angelo was excited at the prospect of going through the waters of baptism, as Jesus had done. His baptism would be a major event in his life. He longed for his mum to be present so invited her to England.

Angelo's mum loved him and believed she knew him far better than he knew himself. When he told her he had met with Jesus and then invited her to his baptismal service, she feared for her son's sanity and agreed instantly to come to England. On arrival and speaking with Angelo, she was determined more than ever to stop him from committing heresy, as she believed his change of heart to be. She'd brought him up in the faith of her family and didn't want any of her children to abandon her belief.

Angelo had changed. He was not the renegade son she'd known and loved. Spending a few days with her boy, she saw in him a change beyond expectation; a transformation she thought could not have occurred unless someone had interfered somehow with his mind. She firmly believed he had been brain washed. Determined to expose the manipulators, she jumped at the chance when he invited her to a meeting of the Alpha Course. Rejecting the idea that any human had brain washed him, Angelo readily confessed that Jesus the Christ alone had purified his heart, body and soul.

Everyone was thrilled to see his mother and warmly welcomed her. As she spoke no English, Angelo translated.

'Would you like a drink? Tea, coffee or fruit juice,' asked a participant.

'No!' came the curt reply. Fearing it might have been spiked, she refused to take anything offered. Sitting next to Angelo she whispered, 'They've put tablets or something in those drinks.'

'No, Mum. There's no such thing in any of the drinks.'

'They'll not get me to drink anything.' Suspiciously, she watched to see if those who drank the coffee, tea or fruit juice acted differently from those who had none and then went on to watch a video about Jesus. Despite Angelo translating the words, she retained her fixed opinion. *What sort of religion is this?* She genuinely thought the church he attended was satanic. 'What's so special about this religion? What's the difference between mine and yours?' she asked.

'It's not a religion, Mum. Jesus is the centre of my life. I speak to Him, and He with me. I have a personal relationship with Him.' His mum was the first person he'd witnessed to in his native tongue. He depended totally on Jesus to give him the right words to say. She started to understand and asked many questions.

The days immediately prior to his baptism, Angelo felt troubled and confided in John. 'Something is going to happen in the church at my baptism.'

'Such as?'

'I don't know, but I'm sure of it.'

John smiled reassuringly 'Enjoy the day, Angelo. Enjoy the day.'

On the day of his baptism, he was ready for anything that Jesus would bestow on him. He was thrilled that some members of his family were there to witness the occasion, especially his mother. There was lots of worship in song and then the preacher gave a short word. The time for Angelo to be baptised by total immersion had come. The minister and an assistant stood waist high in water in the baptistry. Another stood nearby ready to wrap a towel around him when stepping from the water.

Well before the baptism, those nearby sensed that Angelo's mother was uneasy. Her body language and facial expression projected her contempt of what was about to happen. Calling out a number of times during the service, she was agitated and greatly disturbed in spirit. When Angelo stepped into the water, she screamed in anguish. Shaking, she dropped to the floor, wriggling as if suffering from a seizure. She wriggled for some time. Those nearby ensured her safety. Angelo was drying himself when she got up. She looked well and sat down for the rest of the service.

Afterwards, she told him what had happened adding, 'When I got off the floor I felt at peace.'

'I sense an unclean spirit has left you Mum, and that the Lord has touched your heart.' These were brave words to say, but she accepted his comment without any malice. Despite the momentary disturbance, his baptism had been a wonderful event. Angelo felt ready to do God's bidding.

Returning to Italy, his mother was not sure what to make of his transformation. When he telephoned her, she always questioned him about his faith. Sometimes they talked for an hour. Often he would read his Bible to her and then explain its meaning. 'You shouldn't pray to the saints, Mum.'

'Why not?'

'Jesus Christ is the only way to God. No other can mediate for us. Jesus is my best Friend. Put your trust in Him, Mum. He loves you as much as he loves me. Think about it, Mum. Jesus said: "*I am the way and the truth and the life. No one comes to the Father except through Me.*"'

She loved the times he read the Psalms to her. In particular she loved Psalm 23.

The LORD is my shepherd; I shall not be in want. He makes me lie down in green pastures, he leads me beside quiet waters, he restores my soul. He guides me in paths of righteousness for his name's sake. Even though I walk through the valley of the shadow of death, I will fear no evil, for you are with me; your rod and your staff, they comfort me. You prepare a table before me in the presence of my enemies. You anoint my head with oil; my cup overflows. Surely goodness and love will follow me all the days of my life, and I will dwell in the house of the LORD for ever.

During one telephone conversation, his mum said, 'I've stopped praying to the saints and go to church every Sunday. I now pray to Jesus.'

'Wonderful, Mum! That's wonderful!'

Angelo enjoyed reading his Bible. He'd read what the apostle Paul had said, *'When I want to do good, evil is there right beside me'* (Romans 7:21). Aware that his vices were only a moment of weakness away, he sought earnestly to protect himself by wearing the spiritual armour described in the New Testament (Ephesians 6). Around his waist, he wrapped a belt of truth. To protect his chest he adorned the breastplate of righteousness. His feet were fitted with the readiness that comes from the gospel of peace. On his arm hung a shield of faith with which he could extinguish all the flaming arrows of the evil one. On his head was the helmet of salvation. In his hand, he held the sword of the Spirit, which is the Word of God, all freely available and individually tailored by a master artisan. He had no armour to protect the back. He knew that those who wear this armour ought not to turn and run. He had not yet fully realised that his fight is a spiritual battle and not a bodily conflict.

Gill, Marina and their Venezuelan friend Zoraida were praying in the Spirit at Marina's hotel when Angelo joined them. He was saying the Lord's Prayer melodiously in Italian when suddenly he started praying in a new language. Amazed, he fell to his knees, crying. A peace flowed through him. He felt relaxed and joyous. The three women were surprised, but knew the Holy Spirit had touched him. Saved, baptised and now born of the Spirit, he'd experienced the Presence of the Comforter, the Holy Spirit. He wanted more and like Marina, he questioned, 'What next, Jesus?' Indeed! What next did Jesus have in store for him?

Angelo's own comments: In a dark world likened to a vast black forest, I was the last person for God to put me first. 'I'm yours, God. I'm yours, Jesus.' After meeting Jesus, things were different but I still gambled once or twice. Then I listened to His voice and stopped gambling. I prayed, 'If you are real, make me stop drinking.' I loved beer but whenever I drank it, I felt it was like poison. I tried the next day to drink a beer and wanted to vomit. I felt disgust and stopped drinking. I tried again. It was hot in the kitchen so I had a small sip of beer and left the rest. Every time I drank the stuff, I felt disgusted and had lots of pain in my stomach. I stopped drinking even soft drinks. I drink only water and coffee. Guests offer me a drink of wine. I feel dizzy - even when I drink only a little bit.

Before Jesus touched me, I believed the Bible was just a story - a fairy tale - fiction. I hated going to church. God showed me not to follow any person but Jesus. I was a novice; the last person that Jesus would want, but he put me first. I asked for a miracle, a sign. I questioned if it was all my imagination; an illusion or just thoughts in my mind. I'd stopped gambling, stopped smoking and drinking. Were they not enough signs?

When the Holy Spirit filled me I knew that everything I had read was true. This was confirmation that was truly a mind-blowing experience; so amazing. I find the best time for me to read my Bible is when I'm in the bath. It's quiet with no disturbances. I can lie there for hours resting my foot on the hot tap; turning it on whenever the water gets cold. It's a time for me to speak with Jesus and to listen to his voice. Sometimes when I'm busy I don't get a chance to read my Bible as often as I should. It's in these times that I feel drained and in need of spiritual renewal. I always feel refreshed and spiritually uplifted after reading His word and praying. Before I accepted Jesus as my Saviour, I never read any book. Even now, I intend to read one and sometimes try, but my mind wanders on to work or jobs I must do. It's different when I read the Bible.

Jesus shows me love, friendship and kindness. I have a great time communicating with Him. I read my Bible to form a relationship with Jesus and to be in contact with my Best Friend. I usually read a small part and then let Jesus speak to me to reveal His will.

How I ever lived without Jesus, I just don't know. I especially love His promise to me in Psalm 121 where it says: He will not let your foot slip - he who watches over you will not slumber. Indeed, he who watches over Israel will not slumber or sleep. The Lord watches over you - the Lord is your shade at your right hand; the sun will not harm you by day, nor the moon by night. The Lord will keep you from all harm - he will watch over your coming and going both now and forevermore.

13
Doing His Will

Throughout his life, Angelo had met many people. Some were strangers passing by while others popped into his life and out again and were quickly forgotten. But there were those special few who, whether passers-by, brief acquaintances or long-term friends, had something about them that made a lasting impression on his life. They were remembered for a simple word, a kindly act or some thoughtful advice. Ali was one such person who God sent, directed and led to befriend Angelo. Leading a busy life, Ali lived many miles away and was not readily available to pop in and out of Angelo's life so easily. A simple request for prayer when struggling to stop drinking had sealed their friendship.

Ali had arrived in England in the sixties with his Pakistani parents. His mother read the Koran and his father occasionally took him to the local mosque. He was fourteen years old when his father died of cancer. Without a strong hand to guide him through his formative years, grief stricken and unsure of how to deal with such bereavement, he became involved in drink and drugs.

Like Angelo, with no interest in God, Ali was another renegade from all things godly. When in his late teens, a missionary working in his area invited him to watch two videos: one of Billy Graham and the second a film entitled, 'The Cross and the Switchblade'. After viewing, he concluded that if Jesus was real and could change his life, then that was good enough for him. Taking a step in faith, he asked Jesus into his life and quickly discovered that Jesus was no myth but a lifesaver and changer of lives. From that moment, he had a deep passion to tell people about Jesus and a real desire to help those whose lives were broken.

The first few years were difficult for Ali. His family did not understand why he loved Jesus and found it hard to accept. Many intense arguments broke out between him and his kin. He knew that God's love was far stronger than man's hatred for him. He found that human words cannot describe adequately the peace, love and joy a believer experiences when speaking to an all-embracing, loving Creator God. His desire was that his mother would one day let Jesus into her life. He prayed hard to see that day. God answered his prayer when his mum opened her heart to Jesus.

Ali attended a local church and was baptised. As the years slipped by, God called him to study His Word. In obedience, he completed a course at a Bible College.

When first entering Britain, he completely neglected Asian culture. Since knowing Jesus he began to observe a deep sadness in the eyes of many Asian people. When he walked along the streets, a love for them so powerful and embracing welled up from the depths of his soul for them. He knew then that God had called him to love and to minister to his own people. With the God-given love came the strength to face many hardships. He prayed, 'Lord, help me to see what you see and feel what you feel.' God showed him that the only way he could bring his own people to the Lord was by letting them see God's love in him.

Ali's own comments: It's a very dangerous prayer to pray: Lord, help me to see what you see and feel what you feel. Because then you see what God sees and feel what God feels about this world. My desire is that when I minister to God's people, they would have a glimpse of the Lord and find great hope and encouragement in their lives.

Ali had seen in his motherland the hardship and persecution endured by those who love Jesus. He longed to see the transformation of those of God's people who were suffering, and for them to find hope and joy while living amidst the persecution they endured.

God could have given him a love for people anywhere in the world. The people of Pakistan, a country barely sixty-six years old, became his burden.

On one particular Sunday, Ali showed Angelo a video of how those who love Jesus are ostracized and persecuted. The video was about people in Pakistan, but it could have been anywhere in the world where believers are persecuted.

Angelo, full of the Spirit and spiritually strong, his heart cried for those people. 'I must go and see them for myself.'

Despite his longing, he was not ignorant of the fact that those who profess Jesus as Lord and Saviour are not the only ones to endure torment. He knew that ever since humans had colonised earth, harassment in some form had been prevalent. He'd seen and heard enough on television how history along with modern reporting reveals that persecution remains active throughout the world in varying degrees; be it physical torture, psychological trauma, mobbing or bullying. The involvement of organised religion along with world authorities, both past and present, could not escape criticism. Like most, he recognised that whatever the reason for driving people and authorities to persecute others, the act of maltreatment debases the oppressors more than the persecuted. Angelo was learning fast that those who love Jesus are increasingly an easy target to attack. He had no idea that between mid 2008 and mid 2009 an estimated 176,000 Christians were killed for their faith - one every three minutes.

What Angelo had seen and heard stirred him to go and hug those who suffer for loving Jesus. His urge to set the world right by telling everyone about his Saviour was quickly challenged when he questioned, *What am I going to do in Pakistan?* All he knew of Pakistan was what he'd seen on television or heard from others. *Bombs, problems and more problems! Pakistan! That's the last place in the whole world I want to visit. There's nothing to see there. I don't want to go, Lord.* It may have been the last place he wanted to go, but Jesus made it the first for him.

A few weeks had passed since Angelo had viewed the video. He'd had no rest. His heart remained heavily burdened for those suffering terrible hardship and humiliation for no other reason than loving Jesus. Unable to shed the love burden, he listened to Jesus and surrendered his resistance to visit Pakistan.

Confident he'd return with his entry permit, off he went to the nearest Pakistani Embassy. 'I've come to apply for a visa to visit Pakistan,' he blurted out on reaching the desk.

A tall thin brown-eyed Pakistani glared at him questioningly and then motioned with his fingers to show his passport. A brief silence followed as the official flicked through the pages; occasionally glancing at Angelo. 'What's your business in Pakistan?'

'I'm going to visit a friend,' he confidently replied.

'What's your friend's name?'

Angelo's stomach churned. *That's stumped me! What do I say now, Lord?* His mind went blank. 'I can't remember.'

The official's eyebrows rose and his brown eyes widened in disbelief.

Silent, his thoughts raced on. *Why does an Italian want to visit a nameless friend in Pakistan? I've blown it. I might as well go home.*

The official's glare intensified and then, without a word, he walked off with the passport; leaving Angelo to think the worst. Despite every indication that he was doing Jesus' will, doubt crept in. His faith was solid. *Does the Lord really want me to visit Pakistan or is it just an idle fancy I've concocted in my mind to satisfy my own desire?* The official kept him in suspense as two minutes lengthened to five. Fifteen minutes elapsed. *It's not looking good. I'm not going.* Angelo was convinced he'd stepped out of the Lord's will; especially when the official returned stony-faced.

Another finger instruction summonsed him to the desk. Elongating the suspense, again, the official scrutinised his passport. No words forthcoming, he looked directly at Angelo as if to deliver some gruesome news. Taking a breath, almost a sigh, he stamped his passport saying, 'Fine! You can go.'

A broad smile covered Angelo's face as he said a silent prayer. *Thank you, Jesus. Thank you.* The first hurdle over, he wondered how many more he would have to jump before landing in Pakistan.

The flight booked, Angelo and Ali left a rainy England for the heat of Asia. The twelve-hour flight to Pakistan via Saudi Arabia was uneventful. On stepping from the plane, the first thing that hit him was the heat. Even at ten o'clock at night, the heat was unbearable - far hotter than he had experienced in Italy.

As passport control loomed ahead, Angelo dragged his luggage to the gate. The passport officer flicked through the passport, glanced at his face and waved him through. Not so with Ali. The officers asked him many questions, searched him and then let him pass.

Ali was overjoyed when greeted by a friend. 'Hi, Imran! This is Angelo.'

A silent acknowledgement, Imran, keen to leave the airport, helped with the luggage. 'Come. I'll take you to the car. You must be exhausted.' Soon they were in the hotel thanking Jesus for their safe arrival. Pleased that Jesus had brought him, Angelo looked forward to what his Saviour would let him see and do. A quick shower and a good night's sleep was all he wanted.

There was no shade when Angelo and Ali stepped into the glaring morning heat to greet Imran. The three shook hands and hugged one another.

'We'd best go,' urged Imran. 'We've much ground to cover.' The three moved at a quick pace.

There was nothing striking about Imran to make people notice him. Neither was there anything about his demeanour that reflected the hurt and injustice he'd suffered. Of average height with swarthy skin, brown eyes, black hair and moustache, he possessed a soft-spoken voice and held a comforting smile. A man of peace, he generated an abundance of love for everyone he met.

Sadly, Imran carried a burden. His load was not the weight of sin that so many needlessly carry. That had been removed the day he'd met Jesus. His burden generated love, compassion and a longing to ease the pain of others who, like him, suffered for daring to say that Jesus is Lord.

A genuine advocate of justice, he longed for the day when those who loved Jesus could freely worship their Saviour throughout the land without fear of injury, persecution or falling victim to the country's blasphemy laws. Imran, Ali and Angelo entered an area of back alleys, poor sanitation and pitiable accommodation: a place where the rejected, the cast out and destitute struggled to survive. Angelo could not believe his eyes at seeing walls of dried cow dung and mud-constructed dwellings. Entering a small room, where five people lived, sorrow overwhelmed him. He tried hard to hold back his tears. Miles from where he could freely proclaim Jesus as Lord without fear of sanction, he experienced the true cost of knowing Jesus. An elderly woman in simple Pakistani dress stepped forward and bent low to remove his shoes.

'No, no, please! I'm fine,' smiled Angelo, not aware of the significance of her action. By removing his shoes, she was showing her respect. Following a few words between him and the woman through Imran, she understood when he said, 'I'm here to serve you - not to be served.' Removing his shoes, he sat on the bed and prayed. Although he'd never sweated in any kitchen. Angelo equated the experience to baking in a pizza oven. By midday, the heat would be unbearable. He wished he'd brought food or some small gift to give the family. Despite all their hardship and suffering, Angelo sensed a Presence; a love not generated by human source but by a loving Saviour. The family, although cast out by society, experienced Jesus' promise when he said, *I will not leave you as orphans; I will come to you* (John 14:18).

The absence of the father figure was evident. He would have loved to share their fellowship with Angelo, but that was not possible. He was in prison for loving Jesus. When leaving, Angelo felt their pain and carried their burden.

Imran then took them to a gathering of over two thousand people. Ali spoke of the Scripture where Jesus healed the woman with a discharge when she touched His garment.

Angelo recalled the day he'd met Jesus. Through a translator he told the gathering how he'd shut Jesus out of his life. He spoke of how Jesus had helped him overcome his addictions. He laid hands on many people and prayed for their healing. He confessed a little fear when praying for the demon possessed.

Angelo was in Imran's office when Ali drew Imran away to speak privately; leaving him with one of the English speaking staff and a frightened young man desperate to seek protection from the authorities. He sensed the lad's fear. The youth was almost grey in colour and shivering uncontrollably.

'Would you like me to pray for you?' asked Angelo through the interpreter. The young man nodded.

Placing his hands on the youth's forehead, he prayed in the Spirit for his release. The lad fell onto the floor as the Spirit took control. His eyes firmly closed, a radiant smile covered his face. Peace washed over him. Calmly and confidently, he stood to his feet. His fear and shivering had gone. Beaming widely, he hugged Angelo.

Throughout his stay in Pakistan, he sensed the Holy Spirit protecting him. One day, he was so thirsty that someone gave him water to drink. He drank it without thinking. A sly remark unnerved him.

'That water is poisoned.'

Up until that time, Angelo had drunk only bottled water. As Jesus was watching over him, he suffered no adverse effects.

14

Not Alone

Imran had suffered and continues to suffer for loving Jesus. He had held a responsible job as an engineer. With excellent prospects as a single man, he had lots of money in his pocket and nice things surrounding him. All that changed when he helped a pal who was in desperate need of cash. Feeling sorry for his friend and not wanting to see him suffer, Imran lent him 5000 rupees which was a considerable amount of money at the time. When the day came to repay the debt, his friend refused. Without documentation of the loan, Imran could do nothing.

Shortly afterwards, a relative of his friend died. The first thing Imran knew of the death was when police, brandishing an arrest warrant, dragged him to the local police station and charged him with the man's murder. Innocent of such a horrific crime and enraged at the false accusation and forceful separation from his mother, he was thrown into a police cell until the authorities could complete their investigations.

Pleading his innocence, his words fell on closed ears. *Surely there's been a mistake. I've done no wrong. It's all a dream.* A well-respected law-abiding citizen, Imran, took refuge in the thought that his many friends would support him and plead his innocence. He was wrong. Lingering for two months in a local cell, with no trial date or any sign of the charge being dropped, the authorities moved him to the state prison to await his day in court.

Weeks rolled into months. With no prospect of an early release, Imran's anger festered. Infuriated at the lies told about him, he became more disturbed and irate when his friends abandoned him. Innocent, denied liberty and with enforced incarceration in addition to his friends' desertion, he sank into a mind-set that dragged him to deep despair. Desperate loneliness and rejection attacked his reasoned mind. In the midst of his torment, a brief light of hope appeared when a brave pastor unexpectedly visited.

'I've brought you a book. It might help to comfort you.'

Imran was in no mood to be comforted. His anger at his plight would not go away. He saw no reason why he should even flick through the pages. He wanted freedom, not words. Embittered, his temper raged and his frustration exploded at his inability to plead his innocence. An angry man, he had no time for God. Oh yes, he'd believed Jesus had died for him, but now he questioned God's existence; especially when everyone seemed to be against him.

Not long after the pastor's visit, with anger raging within him, Imran picked up the book. Fingering the cover, although not really interested in reading it, he thought it might curb his boredom. Flicking through the pages, he started to read. He read it - not once, but several times. Amongst the thousands of words, he remembered only one sentence which leapt from the page whenever he opened the book.

If you are worried, don't pay attention to it, but fix your eyes upon the cross [meaning Jesus].

His mind raced on. If you're worried, don't pay attention to it. How can I not pay attention to such a worry? I'm accused of murder. Of course I'm worried. Imran was almost hysterical with fearful laughter at the memorable wording when picturing walking to the gallows on death row. As for the second part of the sentence - fix your eyes upon the cross, he saw no cross in his cell - only bare stone walls. In no mood to take advice from a writer who'd never experienced what he was enduring, Imran, alone in his cell, reflected upon his dire predicament. Why is this happening to me? I believe in God. What am I doing here? I'm innocent. I have no-one. Not one to ask how I am.'

Despite his anger blazing in the depths of his inner self, those words *If you are worried, don't pay attention to it, but fix your eyes upon the cross,* were not lost but remained high in his thoughts as if ready to prove their worth. Troubled in soul, desperate in heart and weak in body, he could not escape their power. Those dynamic words, *Fix your eyes on the cross* challenged him. That night while in his bunk, he scratched a cross on the cell wall and fixed his eyes on it thinking of how Jesus had suffered and died on a cross for him.

Imran had been imprisoned for almost a year. He'd seen how other prisoners of the majority faith were treated. They had the luxuries of bed sheets, a special place to worship and many visits from their spiritual leaders. Those who loved Jesus had no such comforts. Considered to be apostates, neglect, scorn and abuse was their lot.

Rather than keeping his eyes on Jesus, Imran fought with God. Considering himself to be a Christian, be that in name only and nominally rather than having a personal relationship with his Saviour, he felt rejected, lonely and angry. In desperation, he challenged God. 'If you are God, show me today. Show me right now or else I'll not believe you are the living God.' Suddenly, in the quietness of his cell, he felt a reassuring hand on his shoulder. Someone had touched him. It was no human hand. Aware of God's Presence, he heard the words clearly and distinctly in a soft, warm comforting voice, 'You are not alone.' Infused with God's love, Imran knew without doubt that God was alive and was with him. He'd experienced His Presence. He'd felt His touch and heard His voice. Early the next morning, he invited a number of prisoners to his cell for a Bible study.

'Don't worry if you can't read. I'll read to you,' he said by way of encouragement. At first, only two came to pray, worship and learn what God was saying through His Word - the Bible. Imran, filled with God's love, prayed hard. Soon, over fifty prisoners were coming daily to pray, worship and learn of Jesus. His cell filled to capacity, the message of Jesus' love and hope permeated the prison.

When news reached Imran that the Superintendent of Prisons would visit, fellow prisoners persuaded him to write and request the authorities to provide a place where they too could worship. The letter was brief.

A flurry of activity swept through the prison as the guards, on their best behaviour, jostled the prisoners out into the enclosure in readiness for the inspection. Pushed into line, Imran stood at the end of a row with his head bowed low. None dared raise their heads as the official, accompanied by an entourage of lesser-ranking officers, walked along the rows inspecting the detainees. All was quiet. The Superintendent of Prisons reached Imran. Contrite, his head bowed, he handed the official the paper. Snatching it, the Inspector read the note. His disapproving look changed to annoyance. Imran raised his head.

Anger filled the air. Screwing up the letter, the chief threw it to the ground. 'You Christians! How dare you ask for a place to worship!' Furious, he walked on.

The brave gesture discarded, Imran wrote to everyone he could conceivably think of, including prison authorities, government ministers and officials, requesting a place to worship as enjoyed by those of the majority faith. Weeks passed with no response.

One late night, a flurry of activity outside Imran's cell disturbed him. In barged a number of guards and dragged him from his bed along the corridor to a darkened room. Without mercy, they stripped him naked, manacled his wrists and then strung him on a hook, which was fixed to the ceiling.

'You Christian! This will teach you not to write letters demanding a place to pray!' screeched a guard as the others hurled verbal abuse.

Like a boxer pounding a punch bag, the guards beat him severely. The attackers spared no place on his dangling body. Unable to escape, he hung heavily; his full weight held by his wrists. Conscious of every blow, the more he cried out in pain, the more intense the beating.

Exhausted by their cowardly acts, the guards took a whip and lashed at his flesh while taunting him and laughing at his belief. Imran lost consciousness. At the point of death, the torture stopped.

Unhooked from the ceiling, the guards dragged him feet first along the corridor to his cell; his flayed back sweeping the rough stone flags and his bruised head vibrating as they pulled him along. Hauled into his cell, the guards locked the door; cursing him as they left. Shivering, bruised and bleeding, he lay naked in indescribable agony. Abandoned by everyone, hours passed into days. When he eventually raised himself from off the floor, he begged for water. The response was swift. 'Shut your mouth!' yelled the guards, 'This is your punishment for daring to write to the Inspector of Prisons!'

Not long after his torturous ordeal, the date of his trial arrived. Carrying the marks of his horrific beating, he stood before the judge, took off his clothes and showed the court his broken body. 'This is what I received for writing a letter.'

The case against him continued and at last, the judge announced, 'We find you innocent of the charges against you and set you free.'

The judge's word echoed sweet in Imran's ears. Relief washed over him. *Free! Free! I'm free. But what is the cost of freedom?* He'd been in prison for three and a half years - incarcerated without trial. Yet, since the day Jesus had touched his shoulder and said, *'You are not alone,'* he had been free in spirit.

On the day he left prison, over 150 prisoners had been attending Bible classes and the entire prison population of 165 prisoners coming daily to his cell to pray.

While spiritual liberty within his heart had blessed him throughout the years of imprisonment, on his release the physical freedom took its toll. Shunned by the community, he arrived home to find his business destroyed, his mother with Tuberculosis and the family living in abject poverty with little food to sustain them. Such was their plight; he knew they had endured far more than he had suffered. Believing that Jesus had placed him in prison to experience the hurt, pain and hardship of those wrongfully accused, the anger he'd felt when first confined became more acute. His anger now centred on the injustice suffered by those who proclaim Jesus as their Saviour at the hands of manipulative people and unjust laws.

A visiting pastor saw Imran's anger and said, 'Cool down and fix your eyes on the cross of Jesus.' This was a repeat of the words he'd read when in prison. Heeding the advice, he praised his Maker saying, 'God opened His Heaven to bless me.'

Such was Imran's thankfulness to Jesus for being with him and watching over him, he visited the forgotten imprisoned Christians and cared for their families. Prayer became the key and care the action. Sharing God's abundant love, which flows from the throne of grace, became his ministry. Jesus walked with Imran through the 'valley of the shadow of death' (Psalm 23) equipping him to empathise with those with whom God brought him into contact. To date, fourteen pastors visit each prisoner and their families weekly. This is truly an amazing insight into God's dealings with those who love Him.

It is rare to find someone who is fearless and ready to die for telling others of Jesus' love in an ever-increasing secular world. Imran's story is not complete. The physical and spiritual encounters continue along with death threats. His response is Jesus' directive: *Love your enemies, do good to those who hate you, bless those who curse you, pray for those who ill-treat you* (Luke 6:26-28). He has found prayer to be extremely powerful.

Imran is now happily married with children. His mother has gone to be with the Lord. While free in God's Spirit, he and his family constantly suffer threatening verbal abuse. On several occasions, they've had to retreat to safe houses; especially when death threats escalate to imminent physical danger. In 2011, extremists murdered two of Imran's associates for challenging the country's blasphemy law.

Angelo's visit was almost over. At a gathering of believers, God directed him to pray for three people he'd seen: two men and a woman. He asked if he could pray for them and they agreed. As he prayed in the Spirit, the man, immediately fell to his knees with outstretched hands. Angelo prayed, crying in pain sensing the Holy Spirit's presence. He then prayed for the woman. Some time elapsed before the man stood up.

At a meeting on the last day in Pakistan, Angelo spotted a young man hiding behind a woman and sensed the man's heavy burden. His face projected a spirit of sadness. Angelo laid his hands on the young man and cried out for the Pakistani people as the Holy Spirit took control. The young man fell to the floor and lay there for about half an hour. On opening his eyes, love flowed out of him and he was light in spirit.

Angelo met many lovely people who knew Jesus. Love bubbled from them. His heart was so burdened he prayed that God would help them in their plight to worship freely without fear of persecution or attack. His final act was not one of giving, but receiving. A Pakistani woman prayed for him. He felt loved and strong in the Lord.

He had spent ten days eating the local food without adverse effects. After visiting a restaurant on the last night, he suffered violent vomiting and diarrhoea. His heart was full of love as his body was fast emptying. He was thankful the upset passed quickly.

The question could be asked; why travel to another country to worship God when Angelo could have praised God just where he was and at any time? The answer: God called him there and he obeyed. By showing his love for others, he greatly encouraged them in their faith while powerfully reminding those who suffer that they are not forgotten but very much loved and a part of God's family.

Angelo experienced the love, joy and peace that overflowed from everyone he met. He knew that his visit and those of others uplifted and comforted the people far beyond the hardship they endure.

He was well aware that God does not call everyone to go to other lands, but felt the need to continue to pray for the persecuted, their families and especially the children of those imprisoned or killed for loving Jesus. Neither did he forget the persecutors - that they too will come to know Jesus as their Saviour.

Jesus had shown him what it is to be His friend in an ever increasing hostile world. He left Pakistan with much love in his heart for the people.

He'd asked, 'Why me? An Italian going to these people!' He had his answer - they are brothers and sisters in Christ Jesus.

Angelo arrived back home far richer in spirit than he'd left. He'd seen God's hand in his life and like others before him, he wanted a closer walk with God, to love people more and to be effective in telling others of Jesus' love.

15

Telling Others

Angelo's time in Pakistan had profoundly affected him. Witnessing at first hand the dire poverty which people endure for daring to show their love for Jesus, he'd met those deprived of work, those treated as dross, and those attacked and imprisoned for confessing Jesus as Lord. Yet amidst all the depravity, humiliation and hardship they suffer, each possessed a deep spiritual richness and displayed their strength of character when speaking of Jesus. Experiencing what money cannot buy - the extremes of love - God had shown him love in the darkest despair and on the heights of ecstasy. Angelo felt privileged to have seen such love generated and sustained by a Heavenly Father, Creator God, outpoured upon those who dare to say, 'JESUS is LORD!' He had witnessed the fullness of the meaning of Jesus' words when he said, *Do not store up for yourselves treasures on earth, where moth and rust destroy, and where thieves break in and steal. But store up for yourselves treasures in heaven, where moth and rust do not destroy, and where thieves do not break in and steal. For where your treasure is, there your heart will be also* (Mathew 6:19-21).

Angelo was not immune from the energising power that Jesus gives. Nor did he want to be. Fuelled up to tell others of what Jesus had done for him, he shared the Gospel message with anyone who would listen.

An Italian representative he'd dealt with for many years called at his restaurant. Angelo could not contain himself and spoke of how Jesus had changed his life.

The man listened, and then said light heartedly, masking his rejection of Jesus and eager to escape the challenge, 'Oh, you're one of those peculiar people. You're the second I've met. There's another like you in Scotland.'

Angelo was curious. 'Where in Scotland?'

'Glasgow. He goes to one of those weirdo churches.'

'You must tell me his name and telephone number.'

The man wondered if he should, but Angelo persisted. 'He's called Ivan.'

When the man had gone, he rang the Glasgow number.

'Sure! Come up and see me,' said Ivan. 'I'd love to meet you. You can stay with my wife and me.'

A few weeks later, after a busy Saturday evening, Angelo locked the restaurant door and drove to Glasgow.

Ivan had a similar background to Angelo. Born in Italy, he had arrived in Britain almost fifty years previously, had owned a restaurant, knew nothing of the Bible and had no idea that Jesus had His hand on him. Twenty-five years ago, Ivan had picked up a children's Bible and had read it. He was so overwhelmed that Jesus had removed all his sins by dying for him, had risen from the dead and wanted to be his friend, he cried and cried. Inviting Jesus into his life, he had sensed such love that he told everyone about Jesus and took whoever would go with him to his local church. He even drove a bus carrying those unable to get there on their own. Called to evangelise, Jesus gave him a healing ministry which took him to Europe, Africa and India. Heeding God's call to set up a children's home in

Odisha, India, the orphanage is now the centre of a wider evangelical mission in sharing the Gospel.

He welcomed Angelo with brotherly love. That morning, Ivan took him along to his church. The music was far louder than Angelo had experienced back home. Everyone seemed sincere and happy. Ivan preached and then offered prayer to anyone who responded by coming to the front. A number of people came forward. After praying for them, he invited Angelo to the front and then prayed for him. Feeling Ivan's breath as of a gentle breeze on his face, Angelo dropped to the floor, infused with peace and abundant joy. He felt weightless, uplifted and so relaxed. He lay there for some time enjoying the Lord's Presence. Following a hearty meal at Ivan's home and talking of Jesus' love, he returned home spiritually strong. 'I want to do something for you, Lord. Where is my service for you?' he asked Jesus.

In church, a little time after returning from Scotland, a woman asked Angelo to pray for a man who had cancer.

Why me? What can I say or do? As the service progressed, he felt a force deep within him saying, *Go and pray for that man. I can't. I'm scared to pray for him. You prayed for those in Pakistan. What stops you now from praying?* He shook with fear. *Can't go. Don't know how to pray for him. My English is not good enough and I can't pray for him in Italian. He might think I'm weird. I don't know what to say. I don't even know him.* Angelo closed his ears and concentrated on the preacher's word, but the voice continued. Yielding to the command that he go and pray for the man he approached him. 'Would you like me to pray for you?' he asked, wondering what he'd do if he refused.

Seeming surprised, he agreed with a smile. 'Yes, I'd like that.'

Laying hands on the man and praying in the Spirit, he immediately felt the man's pain. After praying, he introduced himself and left the rest to Jesus. A few weeks later, the man testified that his cancer had gone. Overcome with emotion, Angelo could not speak.

John saw him crying. 'What's wrong, Angelo?'

'I'm so happy that Jesus has answered my prayer by removing the man's cancer. Lord, what do you want from me? How can I serve you, Jesus?'

Not long after that day, a young woman, who worshiped at the church, announced, 'I've been diagnosed with cancer.' Angelo could feel her pain and felt an urge to go to her and pray. He was nervous and hesitant about approaching her. So strong was the compulsion to get out of his seat and do what he knew he had to do, that he found himself at her side. He had no idea what to say. 'I've come to pray for you.'

Surprised to see him standing there, she smiled and then agreed. He stood silent for a moment with his hand on her shoulder. He prayed and then left.

The following Sunday, Angelo was not in church. None of his friends knew where he had gone. He'd taken himself off to pray for a celebrity who had cancer. The National Newspapers had reported her progress with intense interest.

Not knowing exactly where the person lived, Angelo had received an inner calling to go and pray for her. Heeding the call, he'd set off early that morning to seek her out. Stopping at a filling station, he bought a paper and a map. He'd not bought a Sunday paper before but he wanted to know the latest about her condition. Arriving at her village he enquired as to where she lived.

'She's in hospital,' replied a local.

Driving to the nearest hospital, Angelo prayed he would not be too late.

'She's not here,' the receptionist told him. 'She's in the local hospice.'

Finding the hospice, he parked his car and then walked to the entrance.

'What do you want?' asked one of two security guards.

'God has told me to come and pray for Amber (pseudonym). I must tell her He's heard her prayer.' The guards were suspicious. 'It's not my idea to travel over 150 miles to pray for her. Jesus has sent me.'

Another attendant arrived. Again, Angelo explained why he was there. The guards laughingly mumbled under their breath believing him to be a religious fanatic or just a crank who was not quite right in the head. The third security officer left, leaving the two to snigger. Soon the man returned.

'Did you give Amber the message?' asked Angelo. The guards started to laugh again. Something within him stirred. He pointed to one of the guards and, without thinking said, 'If you don't go and tell Amber I'm here, you'll be really ill. This is God's plan - not mine.' The guards' laughter and sniggers grew louder and mocking. He pointed to the second guard. 'If you don't do what God says you'll be ill too. You can see the Glory of God.'

Ending their hilarity, there was a change of mood. They looked serious, worried and frightened.

Sorry, Lord. I can't go in. What am I to do? You sent me here. I came to see her. It's up to you, God. His answer was, *Go now.* On his way back to the car, he passed two police cars heading for the hospice. He parked the car at a garden centre and read his Bible. *Lord, you must send me an angel to protect me.* Reading for a little while, he sensed God wanted him to return. Tucking his Bible under his arm, he walked back to the hospice arriving at around 3.30 p.m. Several paparazzi started taking pictures of him.

There's going to be trouble. Wow! Sorry, Lord. I think there's going to be a problem. It's up to you now. The day was not going well for him. He didn't want to cause a fuss and was the last person on earth to be outspoken. Frightened and really worried at all the media attention, as he walked towards the entrance an indescribable surge of energy stirred within him. He knew the source. Now he walked with confidence and authority. Nor was he frightened. His favourite psalm came to mind: *I lift up my eyes to the hills - where does my help come from? My help comes from the Lord, the Maker of heaven and earth. He will not let your foot slip - he who watches over you will not slumber; indeed, he who watches over Israel will neither slumber nor sleep. The Lord watches over you - the Lord is your shade at your right hand; the sun will not harm you by day, nor the moon by night. The Lord will keep you from all harm - he will watch over your life; the Lord will watch over your coming and going both now and for evermore* (Psalm 121:1-8).

To the left of the path, eight police officers stood behind a barrier. One sternly approached Angelo.

'You've frightened the security guards. They say you threatened to kill them.'

He gulped. 'No! That's not true. I only told him what God wanted me to say.' He then explained how God had brought him to pray for Amber.

The officer's face set. 'Oh, yes, God sent you, did he? I have to arrest you because you've threatened them.'

'I threatened no-one,' protested, Angelo. 'She asked God to send someone to pray for her and here I am.'

'What's your name?' asked the police officer. 'I need your name in case any of the men die.'

'My name is Angelo.'

'Angelo what?'

He told him and then said, 'If I could only pray for her you would see the Glory of the Lord.' A female officer nearby looked intensely at him but without malice or threat. Angelo sensed that she too knew Jesus. 'If you won't let me see her, can I pray for her here?'

'No!' came the stern reply. The officer walked off and after a few moments returned. 'Okay. You can pray here and then go.'

He'd bottled up his feelings for so long, that his heart was pounding as if to burst. Closing his eyes, he prayed loudly in tongues. Suddenly his hands shot into the air as if to let God fill him. A glut of cameras clicked and lights flashed. Such was the intensity of prayer, he cried out aloud and then left.

Viewed with earthly eyes, Angelo had stepped beyond the acceptable; causing annoyance and intolerance on the part of the guards and police. With spiritual eyes, he'd done what many fail to do. He'd obeyed his loving Heavenly Father. While a none violent action, Angelo recognised that prayer is powerful and threatening to those who disregard the Creator God.

We do not know the outcome of his prayer. Nor can we put our own interpretation on what followed, for not long after he had prayed, Amber died. Subsequent newspaper reports and the words spoken at her funeral service indicated that Angelo's prayer and the prayers of others were answered; not that she should die, but that she'd invite Jesus into her life.

16
In His Care

Angelo's relationship with Jesus grew deeper. He'd felt for some time he should close the restaurant on Sundays. Sunday opening brought in welcomed cash to carry the business over the leaner months. Trusting Jesus, he closed the restaurant and spent time in worship, prayer and relaxing. The business did not suffer, as when open, customer attendance increased.

Remembering his promise to cook a meal for Luciano, the fiery Italian, he decided Sunday lunch would be a good time and set a date. He wanted to cook something special and sat in the restaurant ready to welcome his guests. No one came. *Perhaps I've got the date wrong.* Not one to sit around wasting time, he did a little cleaning and was about to lock up when he saw Luciano approaching with a friend. *That's not his wife. And where are his children?* He gave Luciano a friendly hug. 'I thought you were bringing your wife and family.'

'I am. They won't be long,' assured Luciano.

Two more people arrived with Luciano's wife.

'Where's your family?' asked Angelo expecting to see children.

'They'll be here soon.'

More people arrived. At least twenty people were sitting at the tables chatting to one another when another two arrived.

'We're all here now,' smiled Luciano.

'Is this your family? asked Angelo, humorously.

'Yes! It's my family in Christ. I'll serve the drinks and then help you cook a meal.' Luciano served the guests with fruit juice and then helped in the kitchen. The special meal would have to wait.

Someone thanked the Lord for the food and then everyone tucked into regular pasta and pizza followed by ice-cream, coffee or tea. The friendly chatter continued and after eating, they sang gospel songs and prayed while others danced to the Lord celebrating God's love. Angelo loved the family atmosphere and enjoyed the day. When nightfall came, the guests left for home.

As the weeks passed, Angelo took Jesus at his word when He said, *'Ask and it will be given to you; seek and you will find; knock and the door will be opened to you'* (Matthew 7:7).

Desperately longing for his son Rob who was now in his late teens to meet with Jesus, Angelo prayed constantly that Jesus would answer his prayer. He'd also prayed for his mum and family. His son was far from considering spiritual things. What Angelo wanted was a miracle. He'd known Jesus long enough to know that asking is a one-way process. To ask and receive is two-way - the giver and receiver. Having asked he now had to listen.

One day while driving he had a strong compulsion to visit a particular store. He'd no reason to go there. *I've never been in that supermarket so why should I go now?* The impulse grew stronger and then a voice compelled him to go. Parking his car, Angelo entered the shop where a man stood just inside the doorway.

He's a bit odd. thought Angelo. He looks like Old Father Time. I'd best keep away from him.

Others had similar thoughts and rushed by. The man was of average height, stocky build but not oversized. He had large framed glasses, had a long grey beard to mid chest and wore a long sleeved denim-patched robe and tyre-soled sandals. A length of thick, loosely knotted twine hung around his waist and three grey bags hung from black straps looped across his shoulders. Under one arm, he carried a Bible which was half wrapped in a cloth bag. In one hand, he held a long curved staff to which was attached an icon in the shape of a cross at the top. On his head, was an oversized soft grey hat similar to a trilby.

Angelo would have kept his distance but felt compelled to ask, 'Where do you come from?'

'Pennsylvania,' replied the man in a softly spoken American accent.

'What are you doing here?'

'I'm walking around England. I walk all over the world.'

In conversation, he learned that the man lived off the generosity of strangers he met along the way.

He'd lived this way for almost forty years. Angelo slipped him a few pounds and then left. When in the car park, he heard the voice say, *Wait for the man.* His response was, *Why? What's he to me?* The voice was firm. Seeing the man leave the store, he approached him. 'Would you like to come to my place for something to eat?'

'Sure! That's kind of you. My name is Pilgrim George.'

Angelo drove the man to his restaurant and cooked him a meal.

'Since 1970, I've walked dressed like this for about 40 000 miles through 41 countries.'

'Where are you going?' asked Angelo.

The man gave a wry smile. 'Heaven. It's an adventure for the Lord. You discover what He has in mind when you throw yourself into His arms and see how He's going to catch you. Most of us are holding on for dear life to something, and God says, "Let go, and trust me." When I'm not walking around the world, I live at Holy Trinity Byzantine Monastery in Jefferson Township, Butler County. I planned to become a priest. I spent four years at St. Vincent Seminary in Latrobe and then in the sixties headed for the West Coast of America. I got into many wrong things and ended up in the Colorado Mountains. In awe of the mountains' beauty, I started thinking about God who made those mountains. I'm here because God cares about me.'

'Where do you sleep?'

'Outside. Sometimes people take me in for the night.'

'What about food and drink?'

'I carry drinking water and a few nuts and raisins. I use a filter to purify water from clear-looking streams. I wash in rivulets I find flowing under road bridges.'

After the meal, Angelo told him how Jesus had changed his life.

Meantime, while he was speaking of spiritual matters, his son's thoughts were carnal.

His son lived with his mother and worked with his father. Like most teenagers, his car was his pride and joy. The car had just had a new exhaust fitted. As he was driving home from the garage, he suddenly faced an oncoming car. Turning his wheels to avoid collision, down went the accelerator to the roar of the engine. The car reared off the road, shot up a grass embankment, flipped onto its side and then slid twenty yards before landing upside down. A distraught pedestrian, thinking the worst, rushed tearfully to help.

While all this was happening to Rob, Angelo and Pilgrim George had finished their conversation and were praying together. Just before the man left, he anointed Angelo with oil. 'Thank you for your hospitality. I must go now. I'm on my way to York.' Angelo pointed to the road he should take and then took a photo of his guest. Just before leaving, the man turned and said in a muffled voice, 'Don't worry about…' The last word being inaudible, he left.

Strange, thought Angelo. He felt good that he'd fed the man. He was in high spirits, when the phone rang.

'Rob has had an accident,' said his ex-wife. 'The car spun off the road and landed upside down. The air bag failed.'

Angelo felt sick. Imagining the worst, he pleaded with Jesus that his son would be unhurt. A flood of questions followed. 'Is he injured? Where is he now? Where did it happen?'

'He's fine. He's home. He escaped without a scratch. It happened just across the road from your restaurant. The car is a 'write-off'. Only the driving area is intact.'

'Thank you, Jesus. Thank you, Jesus,' said Angelo, placing the phone down. *Is this the miracle I've waited for? What other miracle could there be than for Jesus to save my son's life in an accident?* Ever grateful to Jesus that his son was safe and unharmed, in the midst of adversity, Angelo was thirsty to know Jesus more. *Show me some other miracle, Jesus.*

Dazed, Rob had crawled through the side window of the upturned car by the time the police and ambulance arrived.

Reflecting back on the accident, Rob said, 'When the car shot off the road I sensed someone or something pushing me back into the driving seat.'

Whether the accident was an unfortunate incident and the saving of Angelo's son a matter of fate is dependent on one's viewpoint and perception. Angelo had no doubt that the saving of his son's life was a miracle and profusely thanked his Saviour.

From the age of twelve, Rob had secretly smoked cannabis. At first, the cigarettes gave him a 'high', made him laugh and then eventually dulled his mind; making him feel lazy and unresponsive. Occasionally he got 'stoned,' as he described it. He abandoned the weed for three years and then along with his friends returned to the habit. Mostly they smoked a 'joint' in secluded parts of the town; when at home, he sneaked a drag in the garage. Some time after the accident, he parked up with his pals to smoke a joint. Lighting a cigarette, he found that his lips had no feeling.

'Hey! Your face looks funny,' laughed a mate.

'What do you mean?'

'It's kind of down on one side.'

'Don't be silly.' Knowing something was wrong, he smiled to hide his fear. He glanced in the wing mirror. The right side of his face hung limp. He touched his cheek but could only feel his fingers. *I've had a stroke.* 'I have to go,' he told his pals. His doctor promptly sent him to the hospital. On arriving at the assessment area, he was fearful and distressed. By now, his right eye was dry and painful. Unable to shut it, he held it closed with his fingers.

The hospital doctor looked and shook his head. 'You have what is known as Bell's Palsy. It's a problem with the facial nerves resulting in paralysis of the face.'

'How long will it last?'

The doctor leaned back in his chair shrugging his shoulders. 'Who knows? A month or even three. In rare cases it never completely heals.' The doctor looked again. 'If the condition doesn't improve you'll have to have your eyelids stitched together to protect your eyeball.'

The doctor's remarks, no matter how honestly conveyed, caused Rob to tremble as he visualised spending a lifetime of misery nursing a paralysed face.

The doctor had others to see. 'I'll see you in a week.'

Anxious, fearful and frightened at what the future held, Rob arrived in tears at his dad's restaurant.

'What's wrong?' asked Angelo, seeing the paralysis.

'The doctor said it could be permanent.'

Angelo hugged him. Rob was still crying when he laid his hands over Rob's eyes. Unable to find the words to say to Jesus, Angelo allowed the Spirit to speak; offering up prayers for his son's healing. 'Have faith that Jesus will heal you,' said Angelo, believing it himself. 'He'll heal you. Trust Him. Put Jesus first before anything and anyone - even before your girlfriend or me.'

Rob stopped crying and started to put his trust in Jesus. Within five days, his face had returned to normal. He stopped smoking and wanted to know more about Jesus.

Angelo had asked in faith for a miracle and Jesus had been faithful to answer. He loved his Saviour even more for hearing and answering his prayers. Angelo's own comments: *I learned that I must put God first in everything I think and do. He's my Saviour, and best Friend.*

He was thrilled when his son invited Jesus into his life. Feeling strong, Rob prayed that he would grow in faith and that the Lord would keep him safe from all evil. He'd never read the Bible and needed to stay close to Jesus if he was to fulfil his commitment.

Eager to help those less fortunate than himself, he offered a young man a much-needed job. The man was keen to work and offered to start earlier than everyone else. 'I'll need a key.'

'No need,' said Angelo. 'You'll start the same time as everyone else. I'll pay you weekly. I'll arrange a room for you if you've nowhere to stay.'

'That would be great.'

The lad settled in his new job and then said, 'I'm a bit short of cash this week. Could I borrow £50 to see me through until next week?'

As most people have a financial crisis at some time in life, especially when starting a new job, Angelo thought it reasonable and advanced him the cash. The request for a further £50 became a regular occurrence. Angelo was suspicious. Enough was enough. He refused when the request occurred daily.

Soon the staff noticed the lad's mood swings. He became nervy, shaky and anxious. Occasionally he had hot sweats.

The headwaiter took Angelo to one side, 'Someone has had their hand in the staff gratuities box. We'd best check the till.' Never before had any money gone missing.

Suspicion fell on the lad. 'Have you taken anything from the gratuity box?' asked Angelo.

'Me! I've not been near it. Why ask me?'

Sensing he was not being truthful, he asked him again.

'I've told you. I've not been near it.'

'Are you sure?' Tense silent moments followed as Angelo patiently waited for a response.

The lad was sombre. Not daring to look Angelo's way, his glazed eyes pierced the floor. 'I needed the cash to help me get treatment for my addiction.'

Angelo sensed a lie. 'Treatment! I doubt that. You don't intend to seek a cure. Not only did you steal from me but from your colleagues. We trusted you. You've betrayed that trust. You're fired. Collect your things and go.'

Had the youth been genuinely remorseful, he would have helped him, but he was not. Angelo had not been faultless when young himself and felt bad about terminating the lad's employment. To retain credibility with his employees however, he had no option but to fire the lad.

Later that day, Angelo asked the Lord to be merciful to all addicted souls. Witnessing the destructive effects that cocaine has on its victims, he was truly grateful to Jesus for saving him from travelling a road the young man was walking. 'Thank you, Jesus,' was his cry.

17
God's Timing

Angelo was in his bath reading his Bible when he sensed a need to pray for the Jewish Nation. This had been prompted by reading Romans chapter 11. Verses 25-31 relate to the Jews being God's chosen people through Abraham, their rejection of Jesus and that one day the Israeli nation will return to their God and see Jesus.

Angelo was sad that they had rejected Jesus. Such was his hurt, he wanted to go and tell them what they were missing. His burden for the people of Israel grew heavy. When watching a Gospel service on the internet, he saw an advert inviting people to join a tour to the Holy Land, so he sent for a brochure. When the itinerary arrived, there was only one place left. He booked the tour, but had first to get to Israel. Excited by the prospects of the trip, he bought a return flight to Israel, but sadly, the hotel from which the tour was to leave was fully booked. Try as he could he was unable to find alternative accommodation.

Angelo accepted his genuine mistake in briefly taking his eyes off Jesus when booking the flight. Enthusiasm had blurred his eyes to God's plan. He realised that God's timing may be different to ours. Knowing what Jesus wanted him to do and when to do it, took faith that He would reveal each step of His plan in His time. Young in faith, he wanted things to happen. He knew that God is wonderful! Inpatient, he had not appreciated fully that sometimes it takes years for the things God calls believers to do to happen. He'd not experienced how occasionally God leads believers along a path they feel is pointless. Only when they see the whole picture do they realise He was equipping them in readiness to carry out what He called them to do. Angelo had learnt that to do things out of God's plan is costly. On this occasion, the loss was only financial.

His burden for Israel would not go away. Sensing the Lord directing him to walk where Jesus had walked, he booked a flight and accommodation. Throwing his luggage into the boot of his car, he headed for the airport. With plenty of time to spare, on reaching the motorway, he reduced his speed. Suddenly the sound of a siren filled his ears. Glancing in his mirror, the flashing lights of a police car were for him. Pulling on to the hard shoulder, his heart pounded as a broadly built police officer stepped from his vehicle leaving his colleague ready to pursue if Angelo should speed away. A few decisive window taps was a sure sign that something was wrong. His stomach heaved. A touch of the window button brought him face to face with the law.

'Do you know why I've stopped you?' asked the stern faced officer glaring at him as if he'd committed a terrible crime.

'No,' he replied, with his CD player blurting out a sermon in the background.

The officer peered suspiciously into the car, listening for a few moments. 'Have you got your fog lights on?'

Angelo glanced at the display panel. 'No.'

'One back light is stronger than the other.' The police officer again peered distrustfully into the car. He prayed silently that the man would let him go. The officer set his eyes on Angelo. His face gave no clues concerning the thought in his head. The atmosphere was tense. 'Get your light checked,' said the officer followed by a much welcomed, 'You can go.'

Relieved, he praised the Lord for answered prayer. He drove a fair way before his heartbeat returned to normal. I've only travelled a hundred miles and already the police are on my tail. How many more holdups will I face before reaching Israel?

Parking his car at the airport, he took his suitcase, paid the fee and headed for the check-in. His brush with the law forgotten, the excitement of visiting Israel grabbed him. Checking in was a simple affair. Relieved of his luggage, with his Bible in one hand, boarding pass and passport in the other, he walked the expanse of boarding gates. Not knowing which gate he should pass through, he rested in a chair. Nearby sat a woman dressed in black holding a few books. Angelo was prompted to speak to her. He held back but not for long. His eyes fixed on one particular book. Thinking it was the Torah, he said, 'Mine's a Bible. Is it the same as your book?'

'No! Totally different,' snapped the woman.

Thinking he'd best keep quiet, he read his Bible. Nothing more was said. On hearing his flight announced, he looked to see how far he'd have to walk to reach Gate 206. He was sitting right beside it. Boarding the aeroplane and finding his end seat on a row of three presented no problem.

A thickset man, dressed in black with a broad brimmed hat, plaited pigtails and a big bushy beard came and sat beside him. A nod was sufficient to acknowledge each other's presence. The man nursed a number of books. By his dress, he looked like a rabbi. A woman came and sat beside the man.

Soon the plane was high above the clouds. An hour into the journey, Angelo's tummy rumbled with hunger. His ticket was for flight only with no food. He felt hungrier when the scholar reached for his case and pulled out a packet of sandwiches. Angelo's stomach protested as sandwich after sandwich disappeared. To take his mind off his stomach and more so off food, he read his Bible. He was thankful when a flight attendant pushed a trolley down the aisle loaded with sandwiches and drinks. Moments later, he sat nursing two half slices of bread. Feasting his eyes longingly on the sandwich, he could not take a bite. He felt the Lord urging him to offer a slice to the rabbi.

I'm hungry, Lord. He knew he had to offer him a slice. You are a Christian. Share love. Show him your love for My people. 'Would you like a sandwich?'

The man's eyes widened with a smile. 'No thank you.'

Thank you, Lord. Angelo cannot remember if the sandwich was pork, chicken or cheese. Fifteen minutes later, the scholar opened a bag of fruit and offered Angelo some. 'No thanks,' he smiled, joyous that the Lord had led him to show kindness to His people. Grateful for the sandwich, his stomach rested - as did he for the remainder of the flight.

On landing at Tel Aviv Airport, joyous anticipation of placing his feet on Israel's soil erupted from deep within. Dragging his luggage towards passport control, a burly female passport officer fixed her eyes upon him.

She breathed in, hitched up her belt and touched her gun. Snatching his passport, she looked at his photo then glared at him. She looked again at the photo and then at Angelo. His picture was nothing like who stood before her. His passport photo was years old when he'd had no beard, short hair and was much thinner. He now had wavy black hair, a moustache, a stubby beard, and a fuller face. She hesitated. Flicking through the pages, she paused at a particular entry. Angelo was uncomfortable. He wondered why she was so distrustful of him. He pictured himself on the next flight home. Again she looked at him and then at his passport photo. She drew him to one side and in an unfriendly tone asked, 'What were you doing in Pakistan?'

He had to think. As always, he truthfully answered, 'Missionary work.'

Again, she looked at him with suspicion. 'What's your business in Israel? Why are you here?'

'I'm here to see the land of the Lord.'

She glared hard at him. 'Where are you staying in Israel?'

When he told her a torrent of questions followed. After a time of grilling, the officer stamped his passport and let him pass. Now free to explore the land, he made his way to the exit.

'It's seven in the evening. Where do I go now, Lord? I'm lost.' He had to reach Jerusalem which was over 70 kilometres away before nightfall. Outside the terminal building, he asked a few folk where he could catch a bus or train to Jerusalem.

The advice was, 'You'd best take a taxi.'

A male twice his size wearing a t-shirt, jeans and trainers approached him. He looks dubious. Clearly not a nice man if looks are to go by, thought Angelo. He has shifty eyes and unruly hair.

'Taxi?' said the man in hardly audible English.

Feeling uneasy, he wondered if the man was trustworthy, but before he knew it, he'd asked, 'How much to Jerusalem?'

'400 dollars.'

'Too much.' He pictured the man robbing him or worse, kidnapping him and holding him to ransom.

'250,' said the man.

He was unsure what to do. *Taxi or bus, Lord? Taxi.* 'Okay,' smiled Angelo.

The man grabbed the cases and led him to his car. Angelo's heart sank at the sight of a dilapidated rust box. He'd agreed the price and didn't warm to the idea of being beaten up on a lonely road if he reneged on the deal. The man had his luggage. A stranger in a foreign land and unable to speak the language, Angelo felt more vulnerable than when on first entering England. Stepping into a shabby car there was no way of knowing what lay 100 metres down the road let alone 70 kilometres. He'd asked the Lord to protect him. The answer had been *taxi,* so he trusted Jesus to take him to Jerusalem.

Angelo sat beside the driver wondering what he'd let himself in for. The stereo boomed out music similar to jazz and the car reeked of cigarettes. He watched as the man sat tensely, holding the handbrake with one hand while gripping the key in the ignition with the other.

What's he waiting for? questioned Angelo.

Suddenly, the car in front pulled away. The driver flicked the ignition and shot off bumper-to-bumper. The car in front stopped at a barrier. Down came a window, a hand inserted a card into a machine and then snatched it back. Up went the barrier and off sped the first car, followed by the taxi, hurling him back into his seat. Down fell the barrier almost slicing through the boot. Angelo prayed. Once on the open road, the driver kept faithfully to the speed limit; ever on the lookout for police patrols.

'Music loud?' asked the driver.

'It's fine,' replied Angelo, preferring to endure the racket than enter into a conversation with someone who may not understand him.

Forty minutes into the journey, relief washed over him on seeing a sign for Jerusalem. Soon they were heading for the centre. The car pulled up outside a multi-storey building.

The man held out his hand. 'Cash.'

He paid his fare. Dumping his cases on the pavement, he thrust his telephone number into Angelo's hand and drove away leaving him wondering if the building was his hotel. He entered the foyer thanking Jesus for his safe arrival.

His room was welcoming and well equipped. After a good wash, he stepped into the street to explore and enjoy his first night in Jerusalem. He wanted to pack as much as he could into the next few days and asked the Lord to show him what He wanted him to see. He looked forward to experiencing the culture and savouring the local cuisine. Filled with great expectations he found himself in an Italian restaurant eating pizza. As darkness fell, excited and tired he returned to his hotel to reflect on events and to wonder what the Lord had in store for him the next day.

The following morning, Angelo left his hotel keen to see the sights. *Lord, I'm lost. I don't know where to go.* He started walking and asked for directions to the old city of Jerusalem. Within ten minutes, he'd reached the city wall and entered through the Jaffa Gate. An elderly Jewish man asked if he could guide him. Before answering, Angelo asked the Lord if the man could show him around. The answer was in the affirmative. It would be a full day's tour as he was led through the old city, visiting many of the sites.

Arriving at the Wailing Wall, his guide directed him to the entrance. The attendant handed him a skullcap, paper and a pencil. He donned the cap. As for the pencil and paper, he looked puzzled.

'You write a prayer and place it into a crack in the wall,' said the attendant.

On nearing the wall, a thickset man dressed in black, wearing a hat and pigtails asked him, in broken English, 'Would you like me to pray for you?'

Shrugging his shoulders, Angelo raised his hands, palm upwards. 'I don't mind.' He had no idea how the man knew he spoke English. He closed his eyes waiting for the man to pray.

The man spoke in Hebrew and within 30 seconds, the prayer had ended. 'Now you pay me,' he insisted.

He was shocked that the man had asked for money. He felt the Spirit stir within him. 'Do you think God allows you to do these things? You should not pray in exchange for cash. That's not right.'

'But I have sons, daughters, and a family to feed.' Feeling sad for the man, he handed him a few coins. 'That's not enough. I need more,' complained the fellow.

Annoyed, he gave the man more cash. 'Now leave me alone. It's not the thing to do.' His heart bled for the man. *Is this your people, God? I understand now why you're sad for your people. They ask for money for a prayer.* A little later, he found himself near the Dome of the Rock. *Do I go in or not?* He felt uncomfortable. There was a long queue, so he returned to the hotel to relax.

Early the next morning, Angelo felt confident that he would find his way around Jerusalem. 'Lord, show me where you'd like me to go.' After trekking some distance, he found himself beyond the city walls walking towards the Golden Gate.

He had heard that some people say the Golden Gate is the one that Ezekiel said should be shut until the Prince passes through it. He reflected on Ezekiel's words. *Then the man brought me back to the outer gate of the sanctuary, the one facing east, and it was shut. The LORD said to me, 'This gate is to remain shut. It must not be opened; no one may enter through it. It is to remain shut because the LORD, the God of Israel, has entered through it. The prince himself is the only one who may sit inside the gateway to eat in the presence of the LORD. He is to enter by way of the portico of the gateway and go out the same way'* (Ezekiel 44:1-3).

The gate faced east. Angelo wondered if Jesus had ridden through it on Palm Sunday. He'd read that when the Arabs held the ground (636 to 1099 AD), they'd sealed up the gate to prevent the fulfilment of Ezekiel's prophecy. Believing the Messiah is bound by Old

Testament laws that prohibit Him from coming in contact with the remains of the dead, Arabs had buried their dead in front of this Eastern Gate.

Walking along the roadside, Angelo heard a voice say, *Go and pray at the Golden Gate.*

He could not see how he could get near. The graveyard stood between him and the Golden Gate - beyond the graveyard, a wire fence barred access.

I can't go up there, Jesus.

Go put your hands on the wall and pray.

I don't know how to get there without permission.

He saw a small gate. Fearful, he squeezed through the opening. Placing his hands on the wall, he prayed and then read his Bible. A very powerful sense of peace drifted over him as he read God's Word. He felt calm, yet at the same time - pain. Praying again, he returned through the opening and walked through the graveyard reading his Bible. He'd been seen. *Lord, I'm in trouble now.*

Two police officers had entered the graveyard. 'What are you doing? No one is allowed in here!'

'I'm a Christian and I went to pray.'

'Have you put anything in the wall?'

'No.' Angelo was shaking.

'Passport,' demanded the second officer.

He always carried his passport. Fumbling in his pocket, he could not find it. 'I've left it at my hotel.'

'What hotel?'

He told them adding, 'I was only praying. I didn't know I wasn't allowed.' His stomach churned. Had he been able to show the officers his papers, the questioning may have been more intense, especially if seeing the last country he'd visited.

Nodding his head in contemplative mood, the second officer glared at him. 'Come with us.'

As the officers escorted him away from the gate, he pictured himself spending the remainder of his holiday locked in an Israeli prison.

18
Living the Word

Angelo's arrest did not sit well with him. Each step generated vivid pictures of imprisonment. His thoughts rushed on. *Locked up for praying at a gate. Surely not. This cannot be.* Prayers came quickly as he trusted Jesus to soften the hearts of the officers. They'd walked him a long way. He wondered if a police cell was a real possibility especially as his escorts remained stern faced and silent. The situation was tense.

A further ten minutes elapsed and then an officer broke the silence. 'You can go, and don't come back.'

Angelo was away. *Thank you, Lord. I've done what I came to do.* The interrogation by the two officers was behind him. Breathing deeply, he felt relief wash over him. He was determined not to let the incident bother him. He walked around the city for ten hours enjoying the sites and reflecting on where Jesus had walked. He felt great. The warm feeling first experienced when stepping from the plane flooded back.

By late afternoon, he approached Mount Moriah, where Abraham took Isaac his son, in readiness to sacrifice him (Genesis 22:1-18).

An ornate building, built around 688 to 691 AD by the Umayyad caliph Abd al-Malik now covers the site. Known as the Dome of the Rock, it is an Islamic shrine for pilgrims.

Only a few people were queuing to enter the Dome so he joined them. Suddenly the queue grew longer. That wonderful feeling he'd bathed in moments earlier had gone. Unaware that the inscriptions around the walls deny that God has a son, Angelo felt agitated. Not sure as to his unease, he prayed, *Lord, if you don't want me to go in to touch the rock, then let something happen to stop me from going there.* By now, he was much closer to the entrance. A tall bearded official, waving his hand frantically, gestured that the man in front of him would be the last person he'd let in. Those behind grumbled bitterly. Angelo was quietly smiling. He'd asked for an answer and got one. Content, he left - never to return.

After a good night's sleep, he tucked his passport into his pocket and prayed, *Lord lead me to where you want me to go.* He found himself at the Garden Tomb and sat soaking up the atmosphere. *The place is so peaceful.* He joined a group of tourists listening to an American custodian speaking of Christ's death and resurrection. Angelo sensed the place was as John's gospel described it. Praying, he felt good. He smiled when seeing a sign over the tomb 'He is not here. For He is risen.' Stepping inside the tomb, he felt at peace. He recalled reading in his Bible how an angel had said to the women who had come to anoint the body, *'Do not be afraid, for I know that you are looking for Jesus, who was crucified. He is not here; he has risen, just as he said. Come and see the place where he lay. Then go quickly and tell his disciples: "He has risen from the dead and is going ahead of you into Galilee. There you will see him." Now I have told you'* (Mathew 28:5-7).

Angelo then visited 'the place of the skull' where it is thought Jesus was crucified. A time for quiet contemplation, he studied his Bible and thanked Jesus for loving him. When leaving he asked a man, 'How do I get to the river Jordan?'

'I'll take you,' he said.

The next day, he was having second thoughts about going with a stranger when the man and a friend drove up to the hotel. Out jumped his guide from an ageing sand covered car. The man spoke good English and his friend had just enough for Angelo to understand. The interior of the car was as sandy as the exterior. Not sure of the two strangers, he climbed onto the back seat. On the way to the River Jordan, the men talked enthusiastically about the Qur'an.

He listened and felt uneasy. *Lord, I'm with believers of a different faith - I don't know what to say. Take over and speak for me.*

After stopping for coffee, they were soon on their way to the southern point of the Sea of Galilee. Two hours later the men parked the car at Yardenit on the banks of the River Jordan. 'Be as long as you want,' said the driver.

The cloudless sky reflected brightly on the shimmering Jordan as it flowed gently south. The riverbanks were green and the trees lining the river were heavy in leaf; an oasis surrounded by desert. Yardenit possessed a tranquillity where troubles could be forgotten and dreams of a peaceful world realised. Watching people being baptised, Angelo reflected on his own baptism. Absorbing the peace, he bathed his feet in the cool water and read an account of Jesus' baptism.

Then Jesus came from Galilee to the Jordan to be baptized by John. But John tried to deter him, saying, 'I need to be baptized by you, and do you come to me?'

Jesus replied, *'Let it be so now; it is proper for us to do this to fulfil all righteousness.'* Then John consented. As soon as Jesus *was baptised, he went up out of the water. At that moment heaven was opened, and he saw the Spirit of God descending like a dove and alighting on him. And a voice from heaven said, 'This is my Son, whom I love; with him I am well pleased'* (Matthew 3:15-17).

Feeling blest he thanked Jesus for bringing him to this point in his life. He knew the tourist board had constructed the licensed site where Christians can be baptised and wondered if Jesus had been there.

On the journey back to Jerusalem, he felt relaxed. Such was his desire to share Jesus with the two Palestinians, he gently spoke of how he came to know Jesus and the relationship he had with Him. The two listened intently. As Angelo spoke, he felt he'd planted a little seed of Jesus' love inside those men. 'Jesus is not a prophet,' he said, wondering what reaction he would get from the two men and then with confidence blurted out, 'He's the Son of God, my Saviour, Lord and King.' His heart warmed towards the driver. He seemed receptive, yet held his own beliefs.

'Would you like tea at my house?' asked the driver.

'I'd love to,' replied Angelo.

His guide drove into the Palestine quarter on the West Bank to a small two-roomed dwelling. There he met the man's spouse and children. The veiled woman could speak a little English. She then disappeared to prepare the food. The children were friendly and inquisitive. He felt welcome.

The house, sparsely furnished with a small carpet, held a sofa, chair, bed and small carpet. The only decoration was a picture of Yasser Arafat hanging prominently on a wall.

'Please be seated,' said his host offering the chair. 'My wife was like you when I met her.' Angelo looked questioningly. 'A Christian, she converted to Islam when we married.'

He felt sad for her and much sadder when she entered the room carrying the bowls of food. He could see the pain in her eyes.

'Please, eat,' he said.

The men helped themselves to cold chicken and rice. 'He's our leader,' said the host; pointing to the picture of Yasser Arafat. 'We love him. We'd have been fine had not the Jews stolen our land.'

Angelo spoke without thinking. 'No! It's God's land. It's not mine or yours.'

The man was stunned at such a fiery response.

Realising he'd said too much, he smiled to break the silence.

'Let's not argue. Come. Make yourself comfortable and tell me your story again.'

He was relieved. 'I love telling people about Jesus whenever I can.' He sat telling his story. As the woman listened in the shadows, he prayed that she would understand. He could see that the family was very poor and struggled to live. 'If you worship the real God, He'll provide for you,' assured Angelo. 'If you worship other gods, you'll struggle in life.'

The man pondered over his words. 'There's a feast tonight. Would you like to come along?'

'I'd love to, but I need to rest. I leave for Tel Aviv tomorrow.'

'I'll take you, if that's okay?'

'Fine!'

'I'll run you back to your hotel.'

When leaving, Angelo thanked him and his spouse for their hospitality and hoped what he'd said would awaken them to the love of Jesus.

The following morning the Palestinian driver drove him to Tel Aviv via Bethlehem. He stopped at the Church of the Nativity. Within the church, is a small grotto where it is said Jesus was born. The queue at the grotto was long.

Lord, I'll not have time to go inside to pray. More people joined the queue. He slipped into the church. A small group walked to the front but a guard moved them back. I *can't wait, Lord. If you want me to go inside, you'll have to show me the way.*

A female security guard had watched him for a while. 'Do you want to go inside?'

He smiled and the guard showed him a quick way in. *Thank you, Lord.* The pressing crowd had little time to view anything. The guides rushed them through the grotto and out in ten seconds at the most. Angelo stayed for ten minutes.

His driver had bought a selection of Palestinian food consisting of very tasty meatballs, salad and bread, which both enjoyed. By late afternoon, they had arrived in Tel Aviv. The hotel was ideally located, overlooking the sapphire-blue Mediterranean Sea and golden sands.

A kind Portuguese woman confirmed his booking, ordered him a rental car and then directed him to a traditional restaurant. After resting, he walked along the coast in search of the cuisine. He'd walked three kilometres and felt sad. *What am I doing here? It's so modern.* Two more kilometres brought him to the restaurant. A traditional dish of fried egg topped with tomato sauce served in a little pan, swilled down by lemonade was a must. Nightfall was not far away. He didn't fancy the daunting five-kilometre walk back to his hotel but the clear night sky and well-lit streets gave him an ideal opportunity to pray. He arrived back at the hotel tired and in need of a good night's sleep.

Next day, he collected his rental car and navigating system which was programmed in English. Typing in his destination, he felt confident that he would reach Capernaum which was two hours north-eastward. Soon he was out of the city and on to the motorway. Half way to Capernaum, he stopped at a roadside café. Returning to his car, he turned on the ignition. 'Oh, no!' he cried glancing at the navigator. 'It's in Hebrew! What do I do now, Lord?' A few coach drivers who were keen to prove their technical expertise fiddled with the contraption. Angelo, amidst a glut of languages, feared the gadget might vanish into some unsavoury character's pocket when passed from one to another. Some time elapsed before a sturdy fellow snatched the route-finder from a man's hand and without too much trouble changed the setting. Relief washed over him as English words appeared on the screen. Thanking the man, he continued into the mountains where his eyes feasted on the vast expanse of the Sea of Galilee. Below stood the city of Tiberius, where, in Jesus' day, Herod Antipas had his capital. Bypassing the town, he headed for Capernaum which had been Jesus' adopted home town.

Much of the old town had been built over, but there were enough ruins to get the sense of where Jesus had lived. 'Mamma Mia Specttacolo!' he cried. 'What a place! Out of this world. The lake is so beautiful!' Angelo was content in the Lord's presence. Sitting on a rock surrounded by the ruins of the synagogue, he imagined Jesus walking there and pictured Him calming the waters and walking on the sea. Late afternoon, he approached a church where it is said the disciple Peter had been born. Seeing a group of tourists arrive he asked an African monk, 'Is there a place where I can hire a room for the night?

'There's nothing around here, but you can stay at my house. There's a small church nearby. I'll meet you there in ten minutes.' Angelo waited and waited. The monk did not arrive. Darkness was upon him and he was desperate to find a place to stay. Trusting Jesus, he drove along a lonely winding road which hugged the sea. There was no sign of civilisation. Suddenly a building surrounded by high walls and electronic gates came into view.

'Thank you, Jesus - a hotel,' he said, thanking Him again when booking a room.

The moon was bright and low as he walked along the shore praying until one a.m. As the moon faded a multitude of stars appeared. *Thank you, Jesus.* He knew Jesus was with him and wrote in the sand *I LOVE YOU JESUS. ANGELO.* Glancing back, he saw words in the sand written in Hebrew and wondered if they said *I love you too*! At one with his Saviour, he slept well that night.

The next day he returned to the synagogue at Capernaum to absorb the tranquil atmosphere and fix his thoughts on Jesus. Fully rested, the next day he asked, *Where are you taking me today, Lord? Back to Capernaum.* Angelo parked on top of a mountain where it is said Jesus had taught The Beatitudes. An American pastor was preaching in an open-air auditorium. The pastor's wife invited him to sit beside her. Angelo spoke of how he'd met Jesus and his love for the Jewish people.

He loved to walk on the mountain, praying and reading his Bible. He was so happy he cried aloud joyously to Jesus as he looked over the villages along the lakeside. He rested and let the Holy Spirit minister to him. Angelo took comfort in Isaiah's words, *but those who hope in the LORD will renew their strength. They will soar on wings like eagles; they will run and not grow weary, they will walk and not be faint* (Isaiah 40:31-32).

The next day he had to return to Tel Aviv. Early that morning, he was setting his navigation system when an image of Mount Carmel appeared on the screen. Driving through the mountains, he reached the top of Mount Carmel and walked - meditating, praying and thanking Jesus for bringing him to Israel.

Sad to be leaving, he arrived in Tel Aviv at ten p.m. He slept well that night. After the airport check-in which was stringent, he sat reading his favourite book. He'd not been there long when the loudspeakers blurted out, 'The airport staff is on strike.' Calm descended into chaos as flight schedules ground to a halt. Many wondered how long the strike would last - perhaps hours or days. But Angelo simply sat tentatively engrossed in his Bible. *Thank you, Lord. You want me to stay a few more hours.* He was happy. This gave him more time to pray for those living in Israel. The strike lasted less than three hours.

He sat unperturbed by the activity around him and wondered where he'd board his plane. When the announcement came, again as on the outward journey, he was sitting next to his boarding gate.

Having packed a great deal into his few days in Israel, he was sad to leave. Thankful the time had felt like a month, he relived his visit for most of the way home.

19
Keen to Serve

Rested, Angelo was keen to develop his business. Passing a large fronted shop central to the town centre, he thought it would make a great ice-cream parlour. The shop was operational and packed with stock. There was nothing to suggest it would become vacant. Abandoning the thought, he concentrated on more pressing matters.

A few weeks later when passing the shop, he heard a voice say, *Go inside and tell the woman that I hear her prayer and she should not worry about it.* 'Maybe I'll go another day,' he said and passed by. The next time he passed that way, the shop was closed. After about twenty days, the shop reopened. Angelo felt a compulsion to see the woman to whom Jesus had told him to speak. Entering the shop, he asked the assistant, 'Why has the shop been closed for so long?'

The man stood silent. Composing himself, he said, 'The shop belonged to my sister. She died a few weeks ago.'

Angelo's stomach burned. Strength drained from him. The day the woman became ill was the day he'd heard the voice say, *Go inside and tell the woman that I hear her prayer and she should not worry about it.* Like others to whom God speaks, he had heard but done nothing. He felt burdened when leaving the shop.

A few months later, the shop closed. He discussed with the owner, who also owned the hotel next door to the shop, the possibility of opening the premises as an ice-cream parlour. However, the shop opened selling leisurewear. After a few weeks, it closed.

Many weeks passed by. Angelo's ice-cream parlour was not to be as he soon realised when attending a church gathering of interdenominational people.

Over the years, many good things had happened in the town. Those churches within its boundaries and surrounding district which confess the Lord Jesus Christ as God and Saviour, had gathered together to proclaim the Gospel by common witness and service for the Glory of God. Not only did they worship together, but arranged regular events to proclaim the gospel.

One such event was a three-day outreach, offering spiritual and practical guidance to locals and visitors. Gospel singers and supporters handed out invitations for free burgers, sausages, tea and coffee in a central garden. Rather than an inducement to hear about Jesus, this was a feeding of both body and the soul. Those seeking to know more about Jesus were invited to attend an Alpha Course. The introduction of Street Angels, Street Pastors, groups sharing God's healing love on the beach and praying over the town were a few activities. These good things didn't just happen. They were the result of listening to and acting upon what God was saying to His people.

Those attending the united church meetings, freely worshiped Jesus through singing, praying and listening to God's Word and sharing in what Jesus was doing. Those with a particular need, irrespective of the reason - be it prayer for healing, seeking God's direction or spiritual gifts, were given an opportunity for others to pray with and for them. On one such evening while Angelo was praying, the building he wanted to open as an ice-cream parlour and coffee shop came to mind. Deep within him he heard a strong voice say, *I want that place. It's going to be opened for me.*

That particular evening, the ministers formed an arch with outstretched arms. People were walking through it praying. The formation of the tunnel had no bearing on God's dealings with His people. Nor was it part of any spiritual ritual, but a spontaneous action to show unity in a diverse religious and secular world.

Angelo stood praying but was sure what to do. The words, *I want that place. It's going to be opened for me,* echoed strongly within him. He walked to the front to ask for prayer and seek God's direction. Constantly praying while walking through the arched arms of the church leaders, he dropped to the ground. Not that he was sick or had collapsed from exhaustion. On the contrary - he was in good health. He was experiencing a pouring in of God's Spirit. The ability to stay upright being too intense, he lay prostrate, immersed in God's love. An indescribable peace flowed through him.

Not long after the meeting, Angelo was not sure if he was crazy or if Jesus was calling him to action. His relationship with Jesus was strong and he knew Jesus' voice. He'd heard Him speak so many times. Because he'd considered opening an ice-cream parlour with a coffee shop, he sensed he was thinking on the side of human desire instead of God's direction. He needed assurance that Jesus was speaking to him and that this was not just an idea he'd conjured up in his mind.

The shop remained closed and he continued to seek for God's direction. 'Oh, Lord, maybe you want this place. If you really do, I need to know it is you who are speaking to me and not some fanciful, whimsical thought of my own. Let me meet with the owner of the property.'

Returning to his car after a morning coffee at a local coffee bar, he spied the owner of the shop standing at his office window beckoning him. *Lord, do you really want this place?* The owner was about to meet with his staff who had congregated around the office door when he entered. 'Come. We must talk.'

The proprietor was surprised when Angelo told him how he'd met with Jesus and that He wanted the place. He had no idea what the Lord had in mind for the building. All he knew was that Jesus was going to use it for His Glory. The man listened favourably and discussed a rent. Angelo left feeling positive. He'd asked for assurance that Jesus was speaking to him and felt confident he had his answer.

The prospects of opening a prominently placed building in the town for Jesus was mind blowing. He had no idea how he would raise the money to pay the rent, but firmly believed that Jesus wanted it for something. One thing was certain; the building would not be a food outlet, ice-cream parlour or coffee shop. Angelo asked Jesus how he would acquire the yearly rent. The reply came. *You don't know whom you are dealing with. I will provide.*

Stepping out in faith, he felt it was time to tell others. John was the first he told. 'If that is what God wants, then that is what God wants,' said John. 'I'll speak with a few contacts.' True to his word, he arranged a meeting of various God-loving people. Meeting at Angelo's restaurant, he told them of how Jesus had spoken to him. The outcome was positive, so they decided to view the property.

The following Sunday, Angelo shared his vision with his local church congregation; telling of what God had said to him. A woman, a little mellow in colour with extremely short hair which was almost crew cut in appearance, was sitting nursing a hard backed notebook. She fingered it lovingly and then said, 'I've just come back from a brief holiday and passed through Glastonbury. I'd not visited before. When standing in the main street all I saw were shops packed with malevolent goods. My heart sank. Then I thought of home and how good it would be if there was a building where people could walk in and hear about the love of Jesus.' A meticulous woman, she opened her book, smiled and said, 'I write down how I feel. Look!' To the right of the page she'd written clearly; *no food - not a coffee bar.*

Months earlier, she'd been diagnosed with cancer and Angelo had prayed for her. He trusted God would heal her. Like so many diagnosed with such a life threatening illness, the young woman had undergone surgery and a course of chemotherapy. She'd prayed, as others had for Jesus to heal her and sought confirmation that healing would follow. She remains well and active.

More than twelve people from various churches viewed the elongated three-storey building. The ground floor had sufficient space to house two shop units and a large reception area. The upper floor which could be divided into two or three areas, was large enough to run various courses, provide a counselling room plus space for a drop in centre - if that what the Lord wanted. Some people agreed to pray and consider the possibility of renting the shop. Others were to seek God's direction as to the use of the building. A meeting was arranged for the following Thursday at Angelo's restaurant.

He felt both humbled and elated without any sense of pride or self-gratification as that is not his nature. He had never considered where Jesus would take him when asking Him into his life. He was grateful that Jesus had saved him from destroying himself. He'd never thought life with Jesus would be so exciting and unpredictable. Over the past months while listening to his Saviour, he had sought and received confirmation that it was Jesus speaking to him and had acted upon Jesus' word.

About this time, an event occurred that seemed insignificant. A burst pipe in the basement of his restaurant flooded the area. He mopped up the mess and lifted a few waterlogged boxes containing old till receipts on to a shelf to dry out.

Angelo knew that although asking Jesus to answer prayers is important, it is only a part of the relationship. Doing what Jesus asked him to do needed courage and much faith. He was well aware that getting it wrong could rouse the people of the world to point the finger, laugh and jeer at him, saying, 'Where is your God now?' He had listened to Jesus, taken a step in faith and put his reputation as a believer in Jesus on the line, so to speak. Success would glorify God. Failure could ruin Angelo's credibility.

20
Disturbing News

Angelo was feeling great, cooking at his restaurant. The next day was the vital meeting. The prospects of seeking God's direction in acquiring the building excited him.

'There's a call for you,' said an employee, urging him to the phone.

'For me?' he questioned with annoyance at being called away from the kitchen. Everyone knew that between six o'clock and nine thirty in the evening Angelo concentrated on cooking and must not be disturbed. His countenance changed from annoyance to concern when seeing the urgency on his employee's face. Taking the handset, he wondered who was calling him.

'Angelo, is that you?' came the anxious voice of his sister-in-law in Italy. 'Your mother is seriously ill in hospital.' His heart sank. 'If you want to see her alive, get the first flight home.'

The conversation was brief. All sorts of imagery of his mum dying filled his mind. For years he'd carried guilt at not returning home when his father had died. This time he would be there for his mother.

The hours until closing time were difficult. His thoughts fluctuated erratically between extreme anxiety and total peace. *Don't let her die, Lord. Please, don't let her die,* was his constant prayer. He'd no option but trust that Jesus would grant his prayer and that he'd be in time to speak with her. He didn't want her to die before she'd asked Jesus into her life. The first flight to Italy was eleven a.m. The meeting to pray and discuss God's plan for the building was to start at ten a.m. Believing that Jesus would let his mother live, he rang John to tell him the news and cancel the meeting.

The phone call from Italy could not have come at a more crucial time. On the brink of doing what he sensed God wanted him to do, suddenly he felt under attack. He began to doubt the voice he'd heard telling him that God wanted that building. He longed to do the right thing for Jesus but was fearful of making the wrong decision. Angelo was deeply troubled when thinking the devil had targeted his mother. Abandoning such thoughts, he trusted Jesus to keep her alive.

It would be ludicrous to think that his mother had any part in diverting him. She lay dying in intensive care. No! His mission was positive. Here was a precious soul to lead to Jesus. He took comfort in the parable of the lost sheep where the Shepherd left his ninety-nine sheep in search of the one lost (Mathew 18:12-13). Angelo knew that while ever his mum had breath she could either accept Jesus as her Saviour or reject Him. Not wishing her to perish, and knowing God was faithful, he continued praying that his mother would remain alive for him to lead her to Jesus. His faith in a loving Saviour, although under attack, remained solid.

Leaving England on a late September morning, he arrived early afternoon in Italy. He was on familiar ground. 'I need to see my mum,' he said on greeting his brother at the airport.

'We can't go now. They won't let us in.'

Despite their mother's critical condition, the Intensive Care Unit stuck rigidly to its half-hour morning and evening visiting times. Angelo hoped, yearned and longed for Jesus to answer his prayers. He desperately needed to speak of Jesus' love to his mum before she died. The hours until visiting time passed slowly. The hospital, which was a large multi-complex building housed every type of ward and department. At one time, it had been part of a religious order run by nuns.

Angelo's patience was sorely tested when sitting with his brother in the hospital waiting area. The pair had arrived at six and visiting was at seven. He sat reading the Psalms and praying. His concentration was disturbed when his brother said, 'Are you ready for a shock?'

What does he mean? Are you ready for a shock? All I want to do is get in and see my mum. He'd never been in an Italian hospital before and had no idea what to expect. He prayed to the Lord that he'd remain strong.

A nurse popped her head around the door of the Intensive Care Unit and said sharply, pointing to a set of gowns hanging on the wall and then to a box of facemasks, 'You must wear a gown and mask before entering. Only two can go in, and remember, visiting time is half an hour - that's all.'

'I'm ready for the shock,' said Angelo as he and his brother gowned and masked. With much trepidation, he entered the room faced by an array of beds. He looked for his mother but saw only tubes, wires, infusion and blood transfusion bags attached to a number of very ill patients. The sound of regular and irregular bleeps of the electronic monitors masked the dulled footsteps of the nurses as they tended their charges. *Is that mum?* he questioned as his eyes fell on her insipid face. *Oh mum.* He felt numb.

She lay propped up in bed. Her dark sunken eyes were closed and her head and shoulders pressed heavily against the pillows. A light sheet covered the lower part of her body. Various coloured wires leading to a monitor reading her heart rate, pulse, breathing and blood pressure ran from beneath her nightdress to a screen displaying the results. In the back of one hand, a needle fed life-sustaining fluids through a clear plastic tube linked to a plastic bag hanging high on an infusion stand. In her other hand, a blood transfusion was in progress. From her nostrils were tubes supplying life-giving oxygen via a glass-bottled humidifier which was plugged into a wall socket.

Ill equipped to absorb the full intensity of seeing his mother so ill, Angelo thought she was going to die that moment. Tears fell on his cheeks. She opened her eyes long enough for him to glean her assurance that she knew he was there. In a room of bleating medico/technological equipment attached to desperately ill patients cared for by gowned and masked strangers, Angelo longed to hold his mum's hand. Fearful he might disrupt the flow of her transfusion, he stood silently gazing at her frailty and prayed. *Heal her infirmity, Lord. and give her peace in her hours of need. Somehow you will allow her recovery so she might come to know you in the twilight hours of her life.* He heard words within him saying, *Don't worry. Your mum is not going to die.* Be it his own deep longing for her to live crying out from within him or Jesus tenderly reassuring him, he did not know. Certainly, the effect of seeing his mother so ill and with his natural emotions running high, he could be forgiven for his wavering.

Time had rushed on and visiting was over. Returning to his brother's house, Angelo could not rest. He walked on the beach praying. There, he sensed a voice saying, *I am with you. Don't worry. Your mum is not going to die. She is going to live to testify to others of My love.* He was certain the Lord was talking to him. *That's good*, he thought. The early morning light was breaking through when he eventually reached home. Resting until evening, he returned to the hospital with his sister-in-law.

A doctor took them aside. 'Your mother may die soon.'

'How soon?' asked Angelo.

'Who knows? Maybe an hour - a few days at the most.'

Recalling the voice he'd heard when on the beach assuring him she would live to testify to others of Jesus' love, Angelo trusted the Lord. Returning to his mother's bedside, he read the 23rd Psalm. She opened her eyes.

'You must go now,' said a nurse.

The next day, his mother showed signs of improvement. As the days passed, she gained in strength and began to speak with him. Whenever he visited, he prayed and read to her from his Bible. She looked forward to his visits. So as not to tire her, he read for about 15 minutes, prayed and spoke about Jesus. The Psalms 23, 116 and 118 were particularly comforting to her.

Hearing such words as, The Lord is my Shepherd, I shall not want, (Psalm 23) and I loved the Lord, for He heard my voice; He heard my cry for mercy - Because He turned his ear to me, I will call on Him as long as I live, (Psalm 116) strengthened her resolve to get well. The words of Psalm 118 in particular, raised her spirit: 'Give thanks to the LORD, for he is good; his love endures forever.'

Between visiting the hospital and spending time with his brother, Angelo sipped coffee at numerous cafes. Old friends were amazed at the change Jesus had brought to his life. Sadly, they refused to admit that Jesus was the source of his transformation.

Since living in England, many changes had occurred in his beloved Italy. At one time, the market place had echoed with the buzz of indigenous vendors. A range of foreign accents now filled the air, each with their own particular tone of Italian dialogue. The land of his birth was changing. Having nothing against incomers, Angelo saw them as souls to whom he could tell of Jesus.

One morning, while sitting outside a café, an African man approached him. 'Would you like to buy socks?' he asked in a polite North-African Italian accent.

He was not amused. Since his arrival, all types of people plying their wares had badgered him to part with his cash. 'Are you a Christian?' asked Angelo, sensing some connection.

'I am,' he replied.

He had doubts. 'Show me your Bible.'

The man smiled and pulled a Bible from his pocket. 'Jesus died on the cross for me,' he said. 'Jesus saved my life. I'm a student selling socks to offset my fees and provide a daily living. Jesus brought you here to help me.' They spoke of their love for Jesus. Angelo refused to buy socks but gave him a few Euros. It was time for him to see his mum.

After about ten days, the doctors were surprised at his mother's progress. By the fourteenth day, she'd improved so much she was transferred to another ward.

21
Love and Pride

The half hour restricted visiting no longer applied. Angelo could stay twenty-four hours with his mother if he wished. The patients were mostly elderly. He soon realised that God was showing him how some carers treat His people. Having never previously experienced the traumatic diversity of needs of those brought low by illness, he'd always thought that carers were as the word implies - caring and compassionate. He was disgusted at seeing how some carers left distraught elderly people to languish in wet and soiled beds: a poor indictment on a profession which built its reputation on compassion for the sick.

His mother was not immune to the lack of care. One day she was struggling in bed to change her position. Angelo offered to help, but she insisted on pressing the 'nurse call' button. After an hour, many lights were flashing and buzzers were still bleeping. She was in such distress that Angelo went for help and found staff drinking tea and chatting.

'These people are going to be in the same position as my mother one day and may suffer more because of their neglect,' were his sentiments.

Opposite was an elderly woman who had just had an operation and was not recovering well. She had badly soiled her bed and was too frightened to call for a nurse to make her comfortable. The woman lay distressed and trembling, staring at her soiled bed linen. A nurse, pushing a trolley packed with clean bed sheets, and dragging a dirty linen receptacle approached the bed.

Help at last, thought Angelo. At least someone cares.

Extremely grateful that the nurse had washed and changed her, the woman profusely thanked the nurse for her kindness.

'If you do it again you can change yourself,' reprimanded the nurse loudly.

The woman cowered tearfully pulling the bed sheets up to her chin.

Angelo was horrified. Hearing the nurse's destructive words, his heart cried out for the woman. The ill treatment of a vulnerable patient in what was supposed to be a caring environment was abhorrent to him. The high esteem in which he held the nursing profession plunged to the deepest depths. His confidence in the vocation was shattered. His understanding of care was that no matter what the condition of a patient, their needs should be addressed with gentleness, patience and understanding. Sadly, the woman was terrified to ask for help when next she soiled the bed. She lingered for a long time in her distressed state.

A few days later, his mother was not well. Her heart was beating erratically with rapid then slow, irregular and missing beats. A few days in the cardiology department and a change in medication brought her fluctuating heartbeat under control. Back on the general ward, grossly anaemic, she received a further blood transfusion.

During those harrowing days, Angelo comforted her by reading to her from his Bible. Patients nearby also listened and requested that he pray for them. This he did. When he read the book of Job to his mother, she could not wait to find out the end of the account.

He was reading his Bible to her when she said, 'I've had such a wonderful dream about Jesus. I didn't want to wake up. When I woke, I thought I'd imagined it. It was real. I saw Jesus on top of a tree. I watched Him look to the left and then to the right as if to tell me something. He did this five times. What do you think it means? I witnessed it all.'

'I don't know what it means, Mum.' Unable to explain the meaning of the dream, he continued to read.

As the days slipped by, his mother grew in strength and came to understand more about the redeeming love of Jesus the Christ. There, in the midst of her adversity, she accepted Jesus as her Saviour; bringing peace to her soul, ease to her body and hope for her future.

Angelo was overjoyed that she'd let Jesus fully into her life and thanked God for answering his prayers. 'You'll have to attend a church when you get out of hospital,' he smiled.

'I don't know about that. How can I? I pray to Jesus, not the saints.'

'You can go to the Pentecostal Church near home. I'm sure the people will welcome you. You'll learn lots about Jesus.'

She smiled, knowingly.

Angelo continued to read the Bible to her. She took great comfort in knowing Jesus.

He spent time with his brother and while praying for his sister-in-law, his brother felt the presence of God's Spirit, and asked, 'Will you pray for me? I want to stop smoking.'

'I can't pray for you tonight,' replied Angelo. 'I'm totally drained.' In the privacy of his bedroom, he asked

God to give his brother the strength to stop smoking. A few days later, his brother developed a cough and amazingly, abandoned his cigarettes for good. Angelo never told his brother that he'd prayed for him. Unaware of the prayer, his brother believed he'd stopped smoking due to his cough. Angelo felt the time was not right to say he'd prayed for his brother. He had now been in Italy over three weeks. His mother had improved so much that he felt he could safely return to is restaurant. 'I have to go back to England, Mum,' he said lovingly.

'No! I need you here,' she said, frightened of losing her source of comfort.

'I must go back, Mum. I have things to do there.'

'I don't want you to go.'

Enfolding her in his arms and placing his hand over her heart, he quietly prayed in tongues. He longed for Jesus to heal her. In those few moments of oneness, he sensed her saying, *Don't pray for me anymore. I'm tired. I've suffered enough. I want to go to Jesus.* After he'd prayed, she seemed at ease. 'I'm going in a minute, Mum. You've improved so much you're going to get better.' His words of assurance along with a beaming smile lit his face. 'I just know you'll be fine.' He hugged her and then kissed her forehead. Hoping she'd not see his tears, he turned and left for the airport; trying desperately to suppress his sadness.

Back in England, he phoned home. His mother was improving. Remembering her dream, he told Marina.

'Jesus is the tree of life,' she said. 'On the left is the wide road to destruction. The road on the right is the narrow road that leads to eternal life. Jesus told us to *enter through the narrow gate. For wide is the gate and broad is the road that leads to destruction, and many enter through it. But small is the gate and narrow the road that leads to life, and only a few find it* (Matthew 7:13-14). Your mum chose the narrow road and met with Jesus. Of that you must be thankful.'

'I am.' Angelo shared with Marina the nursing care he'd witnessed when visiting the hospital.

Listening carefully she said, 'In every profession throughout the world, there are good practitioners and poor ones. The nursing profession is no exception. Some nurses are called to care while others may view their work as a job. The reputation of any caring organisation is dependent on each individual's approach to care when dealing with patients or clients. Every country has its insensitive, hard uncaring people within its caring establishment. I'm sure you've met good chefs and poor ones.'

Angelo agreed.

'It would be great if those who work in caring professions would ask themselves, "Am I in the right occupation?" I don't think that happens. All I can say is, perhaps those who were not so caring, were tired.'

'That's no excuse for poor care.'

'I know. But caring for others is stressful and carers need time to rest, relax and re-energize. Jesus gave His all for us, but He too, while on earth, took 'time out' to receive love and strength from His Father. You know that to express love for others, no matter under what conditions, needs more than monetary input. Love is inbuilt into our character. It's a matter of individual choice whether we let it flow freely or lock it away. No one can receive love unless some other gives it.'

Angelo thoughtfully considered all that Marina had said. He'd been in England for only two days when his sister-in-law phoned him. 'Your mum is getting really bad again. She's not well. She refuses to eat.'

'I'll come back. I might have difficulty getting a flight. I'll drive home tomorrow. I should be there by Tuesday evening.' That Sunday, he went to church and then met with a few friends to talk and pray. Unbeknown to him, sometime between arriving back in England and receiving the call to return home, his mother had experienced the full force of an uncaring nurse.

'Not you again,' sighed the nurse following with hurtful words spoken with venom and much aggression. 'Why do you complain so much? You're going to die!'

That brief encounter was far more destructive than any amount that physical ill treatment could mete out. An unstoppable chain of events was set in motion that day. Having lost the will to live, Angelo's mother stopped eating and refused to have further blood transfusions.

The drive across France into Italy was uneventful. Arriving at the hospital, he dared not think in what condition he'd find his mother. Propped up in bed by pillows as if sleeping, she looked gaunt and her breathing was laboured. He stood at her bedside praying silently. Tenderly, he held her hand. *Oh Mum, you can't die. God promised me that you won't die. You've got to witness to your family.*

She opened her eyes. A smile enveloped her face. 'I'm going to die,' she said in a hushed voice.

'Don't be silly, Mum. God promised me you won't die. You're going to witness to your family.'

She looked at him. Her eyes, which had once conveyed so many messages, were empty. 'I don't know.' She paused, her chest rising and falling as she struggled for breath. 'I haven't the strength.' Her mind was set. 'Take me, Jesus. I'm ready.' With much effort, she spoke of the uncaring nurse.

Angelo felt angered, but love conquered. 'You ought to forgive that nurse.'

His mum raised a smile. 'I've already forgiven her.'

He read from his Bible to her and prayed until she slept. The following day she seemed brighter in spirit, but remained very ill.

A young nurse with eyes sparkling and face aglow approached him. 'I need to make your mother comfortable,' she said lovingly. Tenderly, the nurse bathed his mum, changed her nightdress and bed linen and cleansed her mouth. Before leaving, the nurse made sure she was comfortable and then offered her water to drink.

Both patient and visitor were impressed.

'I hear that you are a Baptist,' said the nurse. 'You are like a Christian?'

Angelo beamed with delight. 'I am a Christian.'

'Me too. I love Jesus.'

Both understood the term 'Christian' to mean having a personal relationship with Jesus and not just a quick prayer of convenience or some mechanistic observance to satisfy the heart or to relieve guilt.

210

From there on, Angelo's faith in humankind was restored. Whenever he saw the nurse, they shared their love for Jesus. She was always in demand, trying to please everyone. The patients loved her.

Two days later, his mother was in so much pain she again asked Jesus to take her. 'Lord, if it's the time, you'd better take over. I've suffered so much.' Quietly, she fell asleep, but before joining her Maker, two teardrops fell to her cheeks. She was at peace. In her final days on earth, she'd accepted Jesus as her Saviour and by doing so had stepped onto the narrow road to eternal life. Earthly pain, suffering and anguish were no more. She'd met Jesus and her eternity with Him was assured.

The days before the funeral, the coffin stood in the front room. At that time, his sister and brother asked for prayer. Many visited to pay their last respects. The priest said the Viaticum, which includes communion and the last rights. Angelo felt uneasy, but knew his mother was safe. He did not want to cause disquiet amongst the family at such a time. After the priest had left, an aunt asked him concerning the Viaticum, 'Did you join in with the priest when he was speaking?'

He shook his head. 'No! I was sharing only when the priest was saying the Lord's Prayer, but not Hail Mary. Jesus is my Saviour and Lord and while Mary was beloved of God, Jesus paid the price for my sin on a cross at Calvary. He's alive and loves me. This is why I can speak directly to Jesus?'

She looked at him as if to say, 'You're probably right.'

Angelo knew that Jesus had given him time to reflect and take comfort and strength from the Psalms he'd read to his mother. He'd learnt when in the depths of personal trials and concentrating on his own concerns, there was always someone he knew or heard about who had a greater need than his. He'd spent hours in prayer with Jesus. He knew that being in tune with Him is like a continuous link, ever open, never breaking down and eternally functioning. Earlier in his spiritual life, through stubbornness and his own free will, he'd ignored Jesus. On those occasions, quickly realising that Jesus never abandoned him, he was soon back on his knees speaking with his best Friend. Now experiencing a closer walk with his Saviour, he had no desire to close his ears and heart to Jesus.

In the short time of knowing Jesus, he'd overcome his addictions, undertaken an Alpha Course, started studying his Bible, been baptised in water and had received the Holy Spirit. In addition, he had prayed for the sick, seen people healed, prayed for the persecuted, walked where Jesus had walked, spoken to many people of Jesus' love and shared with them his personal story of deliverance. He had also watched his son being baptised and had been with his mother the day she had met Jesus. Trusting Jesus implicitly, he'd listened to His voice and no matter what others thought of him, he'd done what Jesus had asked him to do. He'd lived through a steep learning curve with Jesus at the helm. Frustrated by the ineptitude of those believers not tuned to Jesus' wavelength, Angelo longed to know more of his Saviour. This was just the opportune time for that deceiver the devil to strike.

Alone, while reading his Bible in the quietness of his room, Angelo remembered how he'd told people that his mother would live to tell others of Jesus. Now she was dead, he felt foolish. *What will all my relatives and friends think of me?* He felt cold and vulnerable as if hearing the devil laugh mockingly at him. *Your God hasn't done what he said he would do. She's supposed to have lived to testify to the family.*

A struggle was underway - one he must rise above. He'd asked, 'Does the clay question the potter? Who am I to question my Creator God? Isaiah's words came to him. *Woe to him who quarrels with his Maker, to him who is but a potsherd among the potsherds on the ground. Does the clay say to the potter, 'What are you making?' Does your work say, 'He has no hands'?* (Isaiah 45:9). He took comfort in the words: *Yet, O LORD, you are our Father. We are the clay, you are the potter; we are all the work of your hand* (Isaiah 64:8).

Reassurance came when recollecting the telephone conversations he'd had with his mother and how she'd testified to her family about Jesus well before her illness. The seed of salvation had been planted many months earlier when she started praying only to Jesus. When he pondered how family members and others had wanted to know about Jesus, he had his answer. Peace washed over him, as he knew beyond doubt that his loving Heavenly Father held him in the palms of His hand and that Jesus was indeed his best Friend. Like many opponents who play havoc with our lives from time to time, the devil had not finished with Angelo.

At the funeral, he sat quietly in the church cradling his Bible. The last time he'd been in such a setting was back in England with Marina. Uncomfortable or otherwise, he could not walk out of this one. A relative had arranged the funeral. Out of respect for the family, he had little option but to agree to the service being held there. He would have loved the burial service to have been held at his local church but that had not been an option. He knew his mum had met with Jesus so it didn't matter where her mortal remains would rest. Opening his Bible, his eyes fell on Psalm 121 - the one he'd read to his mother about how the Lord watches over those who love Him.

Feeling at peace, Angelo was surprised when, during the service, the priest read the same Psalm! *Thank you, Lord.* He participated when the priest talked about the Father God and prayed to the Lord with him when saying the Lord's Prayer. However, when 'Hail Mary' was said forty times, he silently prayed to Jesus - as when the priest repeatedly said, 'Ave Maria.' He wanted to shout out; *My mum has accepted Jesus as her Saviour. She prayed only to Jesus!* While the priest was speaking, he read his Bible.

At the reception, he spoke about his Saviour to anyone who would listen. Many of his relatives saw the change Jesus had brought to his life. They knew his old ways and were amazed as to how he'd showered his mother with kindness, having read the Bible to her and being there for her.

'You are so lucky,' commented a relative with reference to the change in his life.

He smiled and said gently, 'It's not luck that has changed me. It's Jesus. He can change you too, if only you'd let him by inviting Him into your life. You don't need to look far. It's no mystery. Jesus is someone special. You receive him, and you change.'

Angelo had not seen many of his relatives for such a long time. His cousin and her spouse had driven overnight for seven hours from Rome. She could have phoned to say, 'I'm sorry about your mother,' but she wanted to see him. 'I've given my life to God. I've changed,' she told him. Angelo had noticed. She'd been so unruly when younger. Now her eyes were so alive. 'I still attend church.'

Smiling lovingly, he told her how he'd met Jesus. 'We are servants of the Lord,' he told her. 'We ask for His direction,' and then added gently, 'You ought not to pray to Mary or any saint.' He explained how Jesus had died for everyone's sins and had risen from the dead so all could have life and that Jesus is the only way to God. They talked for a while. She seemed to understand.

'Will you pray for me?' she asked him. 'I've not been well and I'm seeking healing.'

'I'll pray for you, but whether you're healed or not is up to the Lord.' He prayed hard for her.

Not long after the funeral, the devil seized his chance to taunt him. In his solitude, Angelo's all night walk on the sand came to mind. *She didn't get well, she died.* In earnest prayer, he asked, 'Lord, what do you want from me? Is the gift of healing for me? Am I to pray for people to be healed? I don't know what to think. When my mother died, I felt the gift of healing was not the gift you gave me. When people ask me to pray for them to be healed, I pray. I don't want to say any more prayers in front of people asking you to heal them. It's embarrassing. If people ask me to pray for them, I'll pray in private. I don't want the enemy to laugh and put evil thoughts into other people's minds when they don't get healed.' As he listened for a while, he sensed a small rebuke as if Jesus was saying, *She's safe, and has eternal life. What more do you want?* 'Show me what you want me to do, Lord.' He was not to have an answer at that time. Angelo's timing was not God's timing.

He had spent years far from Jesus. In his enthusiasm to seek Jesus' direction for his life, he - like so many who first come to know Jesus - had to learn to identify His voice from that of his own thoughts, desires or mindset. For some, knowing Jesus' voice comes easily. For others it takes a little longer. The more time spent listening, the more His voice became recognisable. Sometimes He speaks through His Word, the Bible, and sometimes through a word from others. Jesus said, *'My sheep listen to My voice; I know them, and they follow Me'* (John 10:27).

Angelo was discovering that when a believer hears Jesus' voice, the time scale to act upon His Word is not always given. He was slowly learning that those who love Him work on GT, (God's Time); not GMT (Greenwich Mean Time) or BST (British Summer Time). God's timing is not ours. Ignoring this, it is possible that an over enthusiastic listener might have a tendency to push events rather than wait for God's directive.

22

Under Attack

The first Sunday Angelo was back in England, John and Gill invited him for a meal. 'What are we going to do with that place?' asked John, referring to the shop that Angelo felt God wanted for His use.

'Well, my heart is saying, 'Yes', but my mind is saying 'No'. It's a constant struggle. I ask myself, What am I doing? Why make problems for yourself? How can you pay the rent? How can you do this? How can you do that? I'm a bit frustrated, because I feel this does not come from the Lord, but the devil.'

'We could arrange another meeting,' suggested John.

Angelo's heart immediately said, *yes*. His mind said, *Why are you saying that? You're not supposed to say that.* He felt his mind was trying to corrupt him. 'If it's from the Lord, it will happen. It's going to be done. Let's arrange a meeting.'

'Can we help to pay the rent? Perhaps we could open a charity shop.'

'I was thinking that if it's from the Lord, He'll provide. He provides for everything. If it happens, it is the Lord's will. I knew right from the start that evil had tried to stop it. Every morning I call upon the Lord to be in me and to speak to me and say things for me, because that's the only way I can do things for Him. I want to do it for the Lord. The thing is, that shop is going to be for the Lord. Who knows? The place might be full of busy people all wanting to be a part of God's action. That would be great! I'm conscious that evil is there right beside me saying, 'It's a big waste of time.

Forget it. Don't get involved.' It's as if the devil is trying to destroy all these things. I listened to a sermon the other day and was refreshed with faith. Sometimes I feel that all the troubles around me are from the Lord to strengthen my faith in Him so I can come out regenerated in His love. If the place is still there, it's because God wants it.'

John smiled. 'Let's see what happens. 'I'll arrange another meeting with the various church leaders.'

A few days later, Angelo, John, the pastor and two others waited for well over an hour at the restaurant for others to arrive. No one came.

His faith challenged, none could say that Angelo had doubted God. Far from it. He loved Him dearly. The problem was natural rather than spiritual. Again he wondered what people would think of him if what he'd told them did not happen. He'd forgotten that God's timing is not fixed to any calendar or mechanical clock. God's time stretches over eons. *For a thousand years is but a day with the Lord* (2 Peter 3:8). The prophets of old knew it and were brave enough to tell the people what God would do. Sometimes it took over 400 years for the fulfilment of prophecy. John's revelation on the Isle of Patmos on the Lord's Day, occurred 2000 years ago and is not yet completed. One thing was certain, if God wanted the shop, it would be vacant if He required it for His purpose.

Angelo was reading his Bible, when he prayed, 'Lord, I don't want to be involved in any alien thing. It's you I love and serve.' Struggling to concentrate, he pictured a friend called Maurice.

Maurice was an active member of the church where Angelo worshipped. In the latter stages of a most painful aggressive bone cancer, he knew his illness was terminal. To human reason, there was no hope for him. Physical death would be upon him earlier than expected. He loved the Lord and was more concerned in the manner of his death than death itself.

A sudden compulsion to pray for Maurice overwhelmed him. He distinctly heard the words *Go and pray for Maurice.* Unbeknown to Angelo, the doctors had stopped Maurice's chemotherapy.

It had not been long since Angelo had told relatives that his mother would live and preach to the family. Jesus was now telling him to go and pray for Maurice. Reluctant to go, he questioned his instruction. *Now I have been thinking, Lord. This is a waste of my time going there and praying for Maurice to be healed. You know it will not happen but Lord, you can do anything you want.* He was having a battle. *Go phone the pastor to go with you.* He picked up the phone. Months earlier he'd prayed with Maurice and was disappointed that God had not healed him. Holding the phone to his ear he said, *I'm not going to do it. I don't want to pray for people anymore - especially for healing. Lord, if what I hear is from you, make me call.* Angelo rang the pastor. 'I must go and pray for Maurice. I want you to go with me. Can you go with me?'

'Sure! No problem. We need to fix a day. He's a bit tired.'

'Fine. Give me a call.'

He was not alone in his prayers. The whole church had been praying constantly that God would heal Maurice. Angelo and the pastor did go and pray with him. Not long afterwards, Maurice slipped peacefully from physical life.

Angelo could not say why some people were healed and others not. *Who am I to question God's dealings with individuals.* He was learning to listen to God and do what He asked him to do. His problem stemmed from a human failing. Pride had weakened his resolve. His credibility was threatened. He'd allowed human thought to take root. When his son and mother had met Jesus he had failed to see or hear the angels rejoicing in heaven. Neither had he considered the effect his witness had on those he'd spoken to - nor the seeds he'd sown in the hearts of those who'd seen the change Jesus had made in his life. How could he? He'd been caught off guard by letting doubt fester and had given a chance for the devil to smile.

Who can criticise? Who would dare scoff at his weakness? Those who love Jesus often fail Him by letting fruitless thoughts invade their thinking. God's love is not dependent on anything we humans do. It is a gift, and is not given in return for anything we have done or will do. God's unfathomable and immeasurable love described as grace is a gift, which although freely given, many fail to grasp.

'For God so loved the world that he gave his one and only Son, that whoever believes in him shall not perish but have eternal life' (John 3:16).

Angelo had faced a spiritual battle and acknowledged his fallibility. Resting in the Lord's Presence, he fixed his eyes firmly on Jesus, renewing his spiritual and physical strength. Failing to shatter his relationship with Jesus, the devil turned to his business to use as a weapon to undermine his faith. Things were fine until an envelope marked 'Inland Revenue' fell through his letterbox. Tax officers believed that Angelo owed the Government money and were to conduct a full investigation of his business activities.

Despite the distressing news, he knew he had nothing to fear and nothing to hide. A face-to-face meeting followed. Two government officials questioned him and his floor manager relating to a seven-year period. They visited the restaurant and checked everything including the till. 'Fantastic! Fantastic!' Angelo was pleased when they commented on how well he ran his business. He felt relaxed and confident that things would be fine.

A month later, he received a letter from the Inland Revenue highlighting discrepancies. Two weeks' receipts were missing. These dated back two years to the time when Angelo had been spiritually strong in Pakistan.

The officers called a second meeting that proved more harrowing. They suggested how much back tax he should pay. The under payment of tax was calculated for the busiest time covering the major holiday period when takings would have been high. The missing receipts covered the winter when customer attendances were at their lowest. He was devastated.

Within a few weeks, he'd received a number of letters demanding sums of around £4 000, £6 000 and £10 000 respectively. Angelo had no idea how to raise such an amount. For years, he'd signed and submitted his tax returns through his accountant and he had signed off the accounts each year as correct. He never thought he'd be in conflict with Government Offices. What complicated the issue was that he had employed three accountants covering the years highlighted for investigation. Never once did he consider blaming them for the predicament in which he found himself. He knew he was innocent of any alleged tax evasion. During the time of the investigation, Ali invited Angelo to Pakistan for a second time.

'I'd love to go, but I have pressing issues I must attend to. I don't know if the restaurant will be closed or if I'll end up in jail. If God wants me to go to Pakistan, He'll find a way, but I don't think I'll be going. My mind is in a bit of turmoil just now. I have a friend in Jesus and He knows I love Him. My battle is with earthly authorities.' Angelo explained briefly his worrying situation. 'I feel as if I'm going through a dark period in my life - much like the valley of the shadow of death described in Psalm 23. I sense that evil is attacking me. Jesus is with me. Since the day I invited Jesus into my life I've been doubly vigilant to ensure I'm squeaky-clean in all my business dealings - financial and otherwise. My integrity, honesty and credibility are under attack. I'm desperate to clear my name.'

Ali offered moral support and prayer.

A second investigation was underway. By this time, only the female official was working on the case and more wrangling followed.

'My heart is clean,' he said, pleading his cause to her. But still the letters came. By now, the bill had risen to almost £19 000. Angelo had no passion to work. He considered closing the restaurant and starting afresh in another country. He was low in spirit and bordering on depression. Closing the business or selling up would not alter the situation. The alleged tax debt would remain and follow him wherever he went. If the demands continued, and he could not clear his name, prison or bankruptcy was a real possibility.

At a particularly low period, he pictured himself in jail preaching the gospel while pleading his innocence. The physical and mental trauma of doing battle with the authorities was telling on him. For almost twelve months, he'd tried to clear his name of any fraudulent accusations. It was now a matter of principle. The trauma continued as the investigating officer cancelled numerous meetings. Angelo had cried out to Jesus, 'Lord, you know I'm innocent and haven't done anything wrong. Let justice prevail and peace return to my life.'

I am with you, was the reply. I hold you in my arms. I carry you.

Despite the reassurance that Jesus was with him, Angelo needed a lengthy time to pray, listen and to seek His guidance. With turmoil persisting and the taunting always present, clear and concise logical thinking was the first casualty. He was in the middle of a raging conflict as the devil sought ways to lure him away from Jesus.

Weary and in need of a change of scenery, he would have gone anywhere to clear his mind and feel peace flow into his heart again. During this tense period, he sensed a call to visit a relative in South America. He had family in many parts of the world, and questioned, 'Why South America? Perhaps to work there.' A quick phone call and off he went to explore the possibilities of moving to Chile.

Things were going well for his relative who owned a large Italian restaurant in the Chilean capital. Married to a beautiful local girl, they had plenty of money, a house and cars. Flying high above the clouds to Santiago, Angelo knew the visit would not be for him, but a time to share the Good News of Jesus with his relatives. Sensing the family was drifting apart, he had to say something to help the union.

On meeting the family, he knew things were not well and was quick to speak of Jesus' love. The pair was receptive as he told them what Jesus had done for him and that while in the aeroplane, he'd sensed that God had sent him to them. They could see he'd changed. His relative remembered him as an ardent disbeliever of all things relating to God.

'Jesus loves you and wants you to ask him into your life. I'd love you to know Jesus. You've got to have a personal relationship with Him.'

His relative's wife wanted to know more but her spouse remained cautious. He was too busy for Jesus. His hectic lifestyle took him away from his family. He offered a partnership, but that was not God's plan for Angelo.

His spouse had a friend in hospital who was recovering from brain surgery. On visiting, she told her how Jesus had changed Angelo and how praying directly to Jesus brings healing. Her friend listened and was keen to meet him.

He was reluctant to visit her. The personal battles he'd had over the past months concerning his honesty and credibility as well as praying for the sick were instilling doubt and questioning his right to pray for anyone. The doubts were very subtle and some came as excuses. 'I can't pray. I don't want her to trust me and then nothing happen. I've no idea what to say. She speaks Spanish. I speak Italian and English. Whatever she says I won't understand. You'll have to interpret, but you know only a little Italian and less English. The Good News of Jesus' love might get lost in all the words? No! I can't do it.'

Despite all his questioning and excuses, he did what he'd done so many times before. He let Jesus direct him. The woman was a soul in need. He knew a believer's mission is to tell others about Jesus. Knowing Jesus was with him, why should he fear?

The woman lay in bed in a single room when Angelo entered with his relative's spouse. She smiled and after introductions and small talk, he sensed that the woman was in pain. He could see it in her eyes and feel it in his bones. She longed to go home. The surgeon had said she'd remain in hospital at least a week and perhaps longer if her blinding headaches did not subside.

'I'm in agony,' she told Angelo. 'My head is really painful. I can hardly bear the pain. My heart is also hurting.'

'Would you like me to pray for you?'

She smiled, answering with her eyes.

Angelo was shaking when he gently held her head. He prayed. It was the first time he'd spoken in tongues publicly since arriving in Chile. He then spoke in English. 'Follow your heart. The Lord is with you. Hold onto Him. He'll never let you go. Be strong.'

A big smile spread across her face. 'My headache has gone.'

'Hallelujah! Thank you, Jesus,' smiled Angelo. 'I may not see you again, but I'll pray for you. Keep close to the Lord, and don't go to the priest for forgiveness or pray to Mary or any saint. They all died. Jesus, God's son, rose from the dead and lives. You need a personal relationship with Jesus. Speak to Him. Let Him be your best friend. He's mine.'

The following day, Angelo received wonderful news. The woman was home and free from headaches. In need of time to pray, he sat beside the blue Pacific Ocean, fixing his thoughts on Jesus. In a local Italian coffee shop, he met a man from Rome and a female national who spoke Italian. Initially they talked about their respective businesses, and then Angelo spoke of his past and how he'd met Jesus. The woman was going through a difficult divorce. Angelo was direct. 'You need Jesus in your heart. Trust the Lord.'

She told him she hadn't wanted to visit the coffee bar, but something had brought her there. She felt uplifted.

Angelo's visit to Chile was at an end. At the airport, his relative stood almost in tears ready to wave him a fond farewell. 'You didn't come here for business but for me,' he said.

'You must thank Jesus for bringing me here. He's the one to follow. Read your Bible. It's a start. I'll remember you in my prayers.' Hugs and smiles followed. A friendly wave and he entered the departure lounge assured that his relative was content and happy.

Arriving in England, the tax issue returned with vengeance. More letters had arrived with the demand having increased considerably. With renewed vigour, he searched and found the missing receipts. They'd been in one of the boxes he'd lifted off the floor following the flooding. Soon, the dried out receipts were in the hands of the investigator.

The inspector fixed dates to meet Angelo and cancelled at the last minute. Unable to prove his innocence, time was passing and the tension rising. Angelo's relationship with Jesus was far more important than money. Jesus had said, *'Give to Caesar what is Caesar's and to God what is God's'* (Matthew 22:21). He had given to God what was God's and as far as he knew he'd given everything required of him to the authorities - including his tax. He knew, had he tried to defraud the government, he would have stepped off the narrow road onto the broad way - the route to destruction. The eighth commandment is clear: *You shall not steal* (Exodus 20:15). He also knew the New Testament verse *What good will it be for someone to gain the whole world, yet forfeit their soul? Or what can anyone give in exchange for their soul?* (Matthew 16:26)

Weakened by months of cancelled appointments and demands for more money, Angelo, not knowing what more to do to prove his innocence was low in spirit. Although he loved God and had fellowship with Jesus, he was nevertheless under attack. His thoughts drifted back to those he'd met in Pakistan who were suffering far more than he'd ever suffered. He'd met the destitute and those in abject poverty. He'd prayed for the sick, the oppressed, the possessed and the rejected. He'd seen people healed and their love for Jesus strengthened. He knew his suffering was nothing compared to theirs. They suffered because they profess Jesus is Lord. He was suffering for an accusation he vehemently and utterly refuted. Had he been suffering because of his faith, the struggle would have been clear and he would have understood the reason. His troubles were of a secular source that not only had the power of destroying his credibility but could also cause people to turn away from Jesus. He was no 'convenience believer' who speaks to God on his or her terms whenever the occasion warrants a prayer. Neither was he merely a club member who attends church to be in with the crowd. Nor was he a purveyor of the right words to say to please the listener. Like many, his relationship with Jesus was fixed at Calvary. He loved Jesus and had access to the Father God. In his anguish and distress, he cried out to God to lift the burden that had plagued him for almost eighteen months. In his prayers, he asked for release and the restoring of his credibility. Lingering in his bath reading Isaiah 54:17, he felt assured. *No weapon forged against you will prevail, and you will refute every tongue that accuses you. This is the heritage of the servants of the LORD, and this is their vindication from me, declares the LORD.*

Reading it repeatedly, Angelo longed for the verse to be an assurance for his soul and an answer to his prayers. There in his bath, he asked Jesus for confirmation of his thinking.

The next day was Sunday. After the church service, his dear friend Gill approached him and said, 'The Lord has given me a verse to share with you.' The two sat at the back of the church. Gill flicked through her Bible and read: *No weapon forged against you will prevail, and you will refute every tongue that accuses you. This is the heritage of the servants of the LORD, and this is their vindication from me, declares the LORD.*

Angelo broke down in tears of joy and praise. 'Thank you, Jesus! Thank you!' God again had been faithful to his cry and pleadings. 'I read that verse last night,' he told Gill, wiping the tears from his eyes. 'Thank you Jesus.'

He had his confirmation. The words, *'No weapon forged against you will prevail and you will refute every tongue that accuses you,'* rang sweetly in his ears. The message could not have been clearer. This was no advice given by a friend to ease his troubled mind. Gill had stated that God had given her the verse to share with him. God himself was saying that he *would refute every tongue* that accused him. God had said, *this is the heritage of those who serve Him* and that Angelo's vindication would come from God Himself. What assurance! Hallelujah!

Enough was enough. He'd been on the defensive for too long. Armed with confidence to face his accuser, when meeting the investigator he felt strong in the Lord.

'I'm honest,' he proclaimed. 'I have nothing to hide.' He'd spent sleepless nights trying to find a way to prove his innocence. The prolonged investigation, the hours of preparation and the numerous haphazard cancellations had caused anguish.

With confidence, Angelo threatened to take the Crown to court for harassment. The investigator seemed shocked at this forthright fearless encounter.

The meeting ended amicably with them agreeing to disagree.

Further harrowing months followed. A letter dropped through his letterbox. Seeing the source, he prayerfully read the correspondence.

I have now completed my check of your return for the year shown above. This is a closure notice issued under Section 28 A (1) and (2) Tax management Act 1970.

My conclusions

I do not need to make an amendment to your Tax Return.

I have now examined the further documents provided at our meeting on (date inserted) and conclude from this that the takings' figure declared on your (date inserted) self-assessment return was correct.

I have notified my VAT colleague of the outcome of my enquiries and he will amend the VAT assessment and penalty (year) in due course.

'Thank you, Jesus! Thank you, Jesus!' shouted Angelo, thrilled that he'd been vindicated of any wrongdoing. The conflict was over. He had rested in the Lord's promise that *no weapon forged against you will prevail, and you will refute every tongue that accuses you*. His credibility as a friend of Jesus was intact. The fight had been with the prince of this world - the devil, and not with the Inland Revenue whose investigators were only doing their job. No celebration followed. Thanking His Heavenly Father, he was aware that those who love Jesus and shun evil become prey to the devil's antics.

Where does Angelo's story end? Well it doesn't. This book is ending, but his story continues beyond eternity.

He is no great orator, preacher or celebrity who people raise to stardom status. He's just one of many who opened his heart to Jesus the Christ, the Son of the living God. Who knows where Jesus will take him next? Perhaps to some remote part of the world to tell others of Jesus' love. One thing is certain, no matter where he goes, he'll never be alone. Jesus' promise to those who love Him is that He'll be with them through the darkest valleys to the ends of the earth. They say there is a story in every one of us. To be meaningful; those stories need to be told to make a difference.

By faith, Angelo, knowing that Jesus died on a cross, bore his sins, rose from the dead, ascended into Heaven and will return one day, had found a new meaning and purpose to his life. He'd questioned, 'Why me, Jesus? The answer was one word - *love*.

By now you will know that knowing Jesus is not a religion. It's a personal relationship with a loving Saviour. No one can prove to you that Jesus is alive. You can feel His Presence and know He is near when you truly ask Him into your life.

It doesn't matter where we come from - the important thing is to know where we are going. Are you certain of your destiny?

If you want to know Jesus personally, why not invite him into your life? If you are unsure of how to speak with Him, turn to the next page for guidance.

Angelo's thoughts about asking Jesus into your life

Knowing Jesus is about enjoying a personal relationship with Him. No matter who or what we are, God sent His one and only Son into this world because He loves each one of us. Jesus died to enable you and me to have union with God. The wonderful thing is that God raised Jesus from the dead! He is alive!

If you really want to know Jesus, think for a moment and then say these words aloud.

Dear Jesus, I know you died carrying all my wrongdoings on a cross so that I can be united with God the Father.

Pause for a moment and think about the things you have done. Your past is between God and you. Then say, Dear Jesus, I really want to know you. I invite you into my life. Please forgive me for all the wrong I have done. I ask that you become my Saviour and Friend. Please come into my life forever. I thank you Lord Jesus, for hearing my prayer. Amen.

What next? Tell someone. Your spoken words often reaffirm your actions.

Start to read the Bible. It's good to read a little each day. The Gospel of Mark is a good place to start. Study each verse and ask Jesus to help you understand the meaning.

Speak to Jesus often. Don't be afraid to tell Him your smallest concerns. Trust Him and ask for His guidance. He's your best Friend and loves hearing from you.

Share fellowship with other believers. Jesus wants you to have fellowship with others who love Him. Find a church where you feel comfortable and holds firm to God's Word, the Bible and where you feel comfortable. Ask Jesus to show you at which church He wants you to worship.

Note: God's Church is you and others who love Jesus. Church buildings are only places where believers meet for collective worship, support, encouragement, and friendship.

You will have read in this book about God's gift - His Holy Spirit. God's Spirit led you to Jesus. His Spirit will help you to become strong in faith and love. Prayer is the key. Trust the action and joy in knowing Jesus is the result of placing your faith in Creator God who loves you.

Words of encouragement. *How great is the love the Father has lavished on us, that we should be called children of God! And that is what we are! The reason the world does not know us is that it did not know him. Dear friends, now we are children of God, and what we will be has not yet been made known. But we know that when Christ appears, we shall be like him, for we shall see him as he is. All who have this hope in him purify themselves, just as he is pure* (1 John 3:1-3).

Conclusion The prayer of the people of this book is that you allow God to fill you with His love and direct you in the way He would have you go.

Blessings

Angelo

Author's Notes

Have you ever agreed to do something for someone and then instantly regretted it? I have - on more than one occasion! Opening my mouth once too often caught me off guard. It happened so quickly. All I said was, 'Would you like me to help?'

Seven years earlier, a short black haired, bearded Italian had slipped onto the back pew of my local church. A quiet man, he arrived late and left the moment the service ended. He continued to slip in and out of church each Sunday morning. To my regret, I didn't take much notice.

Two years passed by, and then friends named John and Gill asked my wife and me out for a meal. 'Angelo told me to invite you,' said John. 'He invites people to his restaurant as a love offering.' You've guessed. The quiet Italian who slipped in and out of church each Sunday was Angelo. My first reaction was, *Why me?* Of course, I jumped at the chance. Who'd say no to a free meal - especially at an Italian restaurant! There were six of us. We sat in an alcove and chose whatever we wanted from the menu. The meal was great.

A few months passed and then, one Sunday evening in church, Angelo who was sitting beside me, said, 'I was in my bath reading my Bible when I felt compelled to write a book.'

I chuckled, silently picturing him up to his beard in bubbles trying to turn the pages of a soggy Bible.

"Why me, Jesus' is the title.' Staring into space, he repeated it questioningly as if speaking to his Saviour.

I knew what he meant. I'd asked the same question many times, *Why me, Jesus?* Angelo fixed his dark brown eyes on me, enquiringly. Instantly, his silent request hit me louder than words can convey, no matter how softly spoken. Not thinking of the consequences, I answered by asking, 'Would you like me to help?' His eyes lit up in the affirmative. A huge smile covered his face. My stomach churned. *What have I let myself in for? What have I said? Wherever am I going to get the time to write his book? Why me, Jesus? Why me?* I was flattered he'd asked me, but hoped he'd forget. The service started and I fixed my thoughts on worship.

After the service, Angelo turned my way and said, 'The moment the title came to me, I thought of you.'

Oh dear. He's not forgotten. My thoughts raced on. *Who am I to dampen his enthusiasm? It doesn't seem right, somehow.* I was just beginning to feel confident in writing my own adventure fantasies. Writing biographies was not for me. Desperate to find a way to say, 'No,' without offending him, I asked Jesus what to do. You're reading His answer.

Ignorant of Angelo's life, the more I learned of him and of those in this book, my faith was strengthened. God treated me to a rare insight into His dealings with those who love Him. Little did I know the problems I would face.

From first picking up my pen to write, I had numerous heartaches that drew me to despair and many more blessings that strengthened my relationship with Jesus.

From the onset and throughout writing I suffered at the expense of computer problems. My computer stopped saving my work, blocked me out and flicked off. On one particular day my screen displayed; *"major fault - cannot recognise partition, disc damaged - unable to repair."* I spent almost a week uninstalling and reinstalling both speech and typing programmes before they worked properly. Then my internet provider link developed a problem. After more frustrating days and lots of prayer, my computer started working.

The cause of my frustrations may well have been coincidence due to mechanical faults. I don't think so! When using my computer programmes for reasons other than writing about Jesus, they worked perfectly well.

Annoyed and frustrated at my time-consuming mechanical problems, physically I was unscathed until I started writing about the Devil's workers.

I'd been writing almost all day and progressing well until I typed the word macumba (a religious cult using sorcery, ritual dance and fetishes). Suddenly my strength left me. My head reeled and my stomach churned. I felt cold and drained. At first, I thought I might be hungry. I'd eaten well and drunk enough tea and coffee to sustain me. I tried to ignore the feelings. The more I wrote about the subject the weaker I became. My eyes fixed on the word, macumba and I shivered. I felt drained - a feeling I'd not experienced before nor wish to encounter again. Immediately I called upon Jesus to protect me. Then, from within me I plainly heard the words, *Turn it off.* Thanking Jesus for keeping me safe, I saved the work, switched the computer off, made myself a coffee and rested. Some time passed before I felt well enough to start work again. I went to bed asking Jesus to watch over me while I slept. I had often asked Jesus to guide my hand before writing. Now I ask Him to keep me safe from unwanted influences, and He does!

Those who put their faith in Jesus need to be aware the struggle is not against flesh and blood, but against the rulers, against the authorities, against the powers of this dark world and against the spiritual forces of evil in the heavenly realms (Ephesians 6:12).

One day, when interviewing Angelo, a strange awareness arose in me. *I know this man.* Then I remembered. I'd moved from another town and was settling down in my new post, when I met with a group of nursing colleagues for a night out. The restaurant we piled into was Italian. I'd never been to an Italian restaurant before. The meal was enjoyable and afterwards we were chatting away when suddenly the chef, servers and assistants lined up against a wall near our table. I guess we'd overstayed our welcome and it was a polite way of saying, 'It's time to go.' There were four of them. My eyes focused on a dark haired, bearded Italian standing between two taller employees. A deep sense of compulsion to tell the man that Jesus loved him surged over me. My heart raced on. How could I tell him? I'd never seen him before. The direction was clear. *Tell him.* Ignoring the voice, excuses followed. *What will my colleagues say or think of me if I do such a thing? They'd say I've gone mad.* Too frightened to open my mouth, we paid the bill and left. Those fleeting moments, 13 years earlier, when I'd failed to act on Jesus' instruction came rushing back to me with both sadness and joy. There was sadness because I'd failed my Saviour, and joy that Angelo had met Jesus. 'Coincidence' you may say. I never re-visited that Italian restaurant or any other until Angelo invited me to his.

Towards the latter period of writing, I needed to interview, Luciano and Ali. Angelo had lost contact with Luciano, so I prayed that Jesus would send him to Angelo. I firmly believed Jesus would direct Luciano to contact Angelo. News reached me that Luciano was in Africa. Not deterred, I continued to pray. A week later, Luciano arrived unexpectedly at Angelo's restaurant. He was leaving for Africa in three days and would not return. Angelo shared a little about the book with Luciano who gave permission for his inclusion.

A window of opportunity opened for me to meet with Ali when Angelo told me he'd be at a Conference 300 miles away. Finding accommodation in the conference area proved difficult and pricey. Paying £60 a night per person without breakfast 25 miles away from the conference centre did not appeal to me. My fourth attempt brought success in the shape of a small farmhouse tucked away in the countryside miles away from anywhere but only a short distance from the conference centre - a twin room including breakfast £65 per night.

The night before leaving to meet Ali, I was desperate to discover if the celebrity I named Amber, had met with Jesus. I checked the backdated newspaper articles on the internet but could not confirm it either way. If I could not verify what I needed to know, I would have to remove a mass of text.

The next day, Angelo and I arrived at the farmhouse. Showing us the breakfast room, the friendly proprietor said, 'I'll seat you next to Debbie.'

Sure enough, the following morning, I sat next to Debbie. We introduced ourselves and then Angelo shared a little of his story. I asked him to tell her about Amber. Afterwards I added, 'I'm trying to confirm if she opened her heart to Jesus.'

'Yes, she did,' came the firm reply.

I looked surprised. 'Are you sure?'

'Yes! I know some of the family. My vicar is the best friend of the vicar who conducted the funeral.'

'Wonderful! An answer to prayer.'

She then gave me the vicar's address and contact number. I was overjoyed that out of a population of over 65 million people with thousands of guest houses, Jesus had brought me, not only to the right place but sat me beside someone who could both answer my questions and direct me to the source of my enquiry. It was truly a remarkable coincidence by earthly standards. To me, it was a tremendous example of how Jesus met my need.

I'd been reading the text to Angelo on a weekly basis when a busy period caused us to stop meeting. A few months elapsed and I was concerned that time was slipping by. I needed to let others read the draft and comment before 'polishing the work'. Angelo rang to say Ali was on a flying visit to Marina's hotel. Normally I would not have taken my Bible, pencil or paper to a hotel, but something deep within prompted me to take them. Ali had brought Imran. Five of us sat in the dining area as Imran spoke. From the onset, I scribbled down Imran's testimony. Like the woman who God had sat beside me to confirm that Amber had given her heart to Jesus, here was a man whom God had sent all the way from Pakistan so I could add his experience to the chapter that was lacking - truly a remarkable occurrence. My growing frustration at not meeting with Angelo to complete the first reading was another lesson learned. It's God's timing that matters more than mine. He had it planned for me to meet Imran long before I knew of his existence. We have an amazing God who sees and knows our needs.

I thought I'd completed the book so asked a number of people to read and comment on the content. Removing about 30 pages from the text, I felt troubled. The book had never been proof read. My concern lingered throughout the time of designing the cover. An invitation to my granddaughter's wedding in Scotland provided a welcome respite. When sharing with a guest a little about another book I was writing, I spoke of the blessings I'd had.

Listening intently, she asked, 'Who is proofreading them?'

'I had to say, 'No-one.'

She sat for a moment and then, without prompting, offered to proof read both books.

I was thrilled. Again, God had seen my need and provided the answer.

I'm really blessed knowing Jesus. He's my Best Friend in heavenly places, yet He's also within me. It's hard to explain, but those who know Him understand.

Bibliography

Why Jesus? 1988 Kingsway Publications Ltd 1991

The Alpha Course by Alpha International.

Simon Eebag Montefiore: Jerusalem the Biography Abd al-Malik – The Dome of the Rock page 181.